Building Together

Building Together

How Relationships Make Families and Communities More Resilient

Benjamin Kearney, PhD

with Frank W. Lewis

The Institute of Family and Community Impact

AN OHIOGUIDESTONE COMPANY

Berea, Ohio

The Institute of Family and Community Impact
AN OHIOGUIDESTONE COMPANY
www.ohioguidestone.org

ISBN 978-1-7328190-1-6

Printed in the United States of America
1.01

Contents

Building Together

Introduction

In the 1990s, endangered white rhinos living in South Africa's Pilanesberg Park were turning up dead. Savagely murdered, in fact. But their horns were intact, which meant this was not the work of poachers. As *60 Minutes* would later explain in a segment titled "The Delinquents," rangers determined that the killers were adolescent male elephants.

These elephants had been born in another preserve, Kruger National Park, but the elephant population there had grown too large. At the time there was no way to transport adult elephants, so the keepers made a fateful decision: to kill the adults and relocate the youngest. The government veterinarian who approved it lamented that there was no other option.

The problem was that this ruined the elephants' socialization processes.

Adult male and female elephants live in separate herds, and the young spend their first ten years with their mothers, aunts, and grandmothers. These older female elephants socialize the young and teach them life skills, like finding water holes and where the bones of their ancestors lie. After ten years, the young females begin to participate in raising the next generation, and the males are sent to live with the herd of adult males. They then go through another socialization process, with their fathers and uncles, and at around age twenty, they may assume leadership roles in that herd and procreate.

When the young, orphaned elephants were delivered to Pilanesberg Park, they were cut off from this process. Eventually a teenage male named Mafuto organized his fellow misfits into their own herd. Their campaign against the rhinos began as harassment—and it was almost comical, because the elephants were so small. But as they grew, and as hormones kicked in, their behavior escalated. Their attacks eventually claimed the lives of thirty-nine rhinos, 10 percent of the park's population.

Mafuto was put down, but the rangers were able to find another option for the rest. Using new, specially designed trucks, they brought in fully grown male elephants, who quickly established a new hierarchy. The rhino murders stopped. The *60 Minutes* report likened the solution to father figures confronting a gang of teenage boys who have been terrorizing their neighborhood.

I first heard this story at a conference for therapists in a presentation by Darcia Narvaez, a professor of psychology at the University of Notre Dame and an expert on moral development. Dr. Narvaez doesn't study elephants, but her interests and influences range across disciplines and she relayed the story to make an important point about humans: We are more like our mammalian kin than we realize. We share not just physical characteristics like organ systems and the need to sleep, but behaviors, both inherited and learned. The most important shared attribute, the one that separates mammals from all other creatures on the planet, is our reliance on attachment to others of our species.

Elephant and other mammal communities serve the same function for their young as human communities do for babies—to mold them into mature, socialized adults. When that process breaks down, the socialization process is interrupted and the animal, or human, grows up isolated, mistrusting, and, often, aggressive. The documentary *Blackfish* tells the sad story of Tilikum, a killer whale captured as a juvenile for SeaWorld, who later injured and killed trainers.

Among humans, the effects of isolation are felt not just by individuals but by groups. We did not evolve from lions and cheetahs, living largely solitary lives. We are much more like chimpanzees, who live in clans. And like chimps, we can organize quickly into hierarchical tribes primed for conflict with other groups. This is an important trait, but it's not a healthy state for us and, when it's prolonged, it takes a toll. Once on a war footing, the tribe spends less time nurturing its young and building relationships, and the sense of community breaks down.

If we could examine the brains of the Pilanesberg Park elephants with the technology available today, we would almost certainly find abnormalities in the sizes of certain structures and their capacities to communicate with each other. These abnormalities would likely be consistent across all the members of the elephant gang, who had different sets of parents. Why? Because experience changes the very architecture of the brain—the hardwiring, as we often call it—and negative experiences force changes that compel detrimental behavior. Experience influences biology, and biology influences experience in equal measure in all mammals, including humans.

We used to believe that we could not grow new brain cells, which are called neurons. As an undergraduate in the 1980s, I was taught that the brain is a black box, that we are born with nothing except a few impulses, and that experience dictates virtually everything about us. Thanks to amazing advances in neuroscience, we now know that none of this is true. Experience does indeed shape who we become, but there are biological processes at play as well, many of them inherited from and shared with our mammalian kin, and we can no longer ignore biology if we are to help people affected by stress and trauma.

In humans, 80 percent of brain development occurs in the first four years. There are additional bursts at adolescence and in early adulthood, but the foundation for the advances in verbalization, logic and emotion processing, empathy, and everything else that we rely on to function in a complex society is laid before the age of five. And that process begins at birth.

There are about 100 billion neurons in your brain with as many as 100 trillion connections, called synapses, between them. The most rapid growth of synapses occurs between birth and age three, but new connections are formed and pruned away throughout our lives, and experience drives all of it. In his book *Behave: The Biology of Humans at Our Best and Worst*, Dr. Robert Sapolsky describes what would happen if you were to wear an eye patch for a few days: Almost immediately, the neurons in your auditory processing area would start sprouting dendrites (the fibers through which neurons connect) to reach to the visual center, to help compensate for the lack of visual information. Take away the eye patch, and those dendrites would stop spreading and eventually will be pruned back because they aren't needed.

Moreover, the brain will organize itself to respond quickly, even if learned responses are inappropriate and detrimental. Uncommon experiences build the synaptic equivalents of dirt roads, inefficient and easily lost if not used. Recurring experiences turn those paths into paved roads and eventually superhighways, designed for speed, volume, and durability. The brain of a child growing up in a stressful environment will build synaptic superhighways around their capacities to respond to anxiety instead of around learning to regulate their own emotions and to forge bonds with other people. If untreated, the child will carry this burden into adulthood and quite likely pass similar traits onto his or her own children through behavior and, as we'll discuss later, through DNA.

At OhioGuidestone, we believe that we are not just helping parents, children, and infants. We are helping their communities and their future offspring. That's why it's so vitally important that we help them make changes in their lives today. The damage is not necessarily permanent. The key to preventing and possibly reversing it is relational attachments with other people. And all of us have roles to play.

Positive experiences compensate for stress in childhood. When a child's experiences are healthy, vibrant, and enriching, in an environment that is rich in opportunities for exploring and social play, the child's response systems are strengthened. The architecture and chemistry of the brain change, reversing the effects on stress hormone output, and helping the child return to baseline on his or her own.

Prevention is more effective than treatment, and so the earlier we can get involved in children's lives, the better. OhioGuidestone believes:

• Toxic stress resulting from abuse, neglect, poverty, and other chronic conditions interferes with the neurobiological processes through which children learn to regulate themselves and form bonds with others.

• We can prevent, mitigate, and sometimes even reverse the damage with intuitive, noninvasive, and relatively inexpensive interventions that help children and caregivers build stronger, healthier bonds.

• These interventions can improve physical health, strengthen families, and build more stable and cooperative communities in the near and distant future.

We have identified eight elements that are key to delivering impact to families in need:

1. Belonging to a social network that encompasses a "we" perspective rather than a self-defining one, such as "us vs. them."
2. Belonging to a social network that has a shared altruistic vision.
3. Belonging to a nurturing home.
4. Engaging in an early-enhanced reading environment.
5. Building and enhancing resiliency.
6. Engaging in nurturing relationships and therapeutic support.
7. Limiting exposure to "artificial joy," like addictions.
8. Addressing the interconnection of mental and physical health.

It's a comprehensive list, to be sure. There are no quick fixes. But all these interventions are powered by a few universally recognized and inexhaustible forces. Chief among them is joy. When we combat adverse childhood experiences and toxic stress responses, all our interventions must be relational, and must lead to joy. That joy process changes the understanding of social-emotional relationships and lessens the impact of toxic stress.

When we build joy processes, we don't need so many rules.

Children are more likely to behave when they experience sufficient joy and care in their lives. So we need to equip families with the capacity to find more joy. The rest will follow; as group mammals, we are hardwired to develop social connectedness. We want to be loved and to love. We just have to be shown how.

This book is not just for therapists. We hope that those who make the funding and policy decisions that determine where and how resources are deployed, and indeed everyone who wants stronger, more resilient families and communities, will heed the message. Neuroscience has advanced more in the past decade than in the previous century. It's time for everyone in a position to help families to catch up. Evolution has given us the most complex brain on the planet, and we've used it to do marvelous things—to touch the face of God, as the poet John Gillespie Magee Jr. once described the miracle of flight. Can we learn to use it to touch each other's hearts and open each other's minds? Can we learn how to build a better future together?

CHAPTER 1

Born This Way: Brain, Body, and Behavior

"We are just an advanced breed of monkeys on a minor planet of a very average star. But we can understand the Universe. That makes us something very special."

—Stephen Hawking

For many years we only looked at behavior from the top down. Think of Pavlov's dogs, drooling in response to a sound they'd been taught to associate with food. But Jaak Panksepp challenged that. A neuroscientist and psychobiologist at Bowling Green University, Panksepp is the father of affective neuroscience, the study of the neural mechanisms of emotion. He describes a bottom-up *and* top-down interaction between the brain and the body, and has presented overwhelming evidence that all mammals are driven by four *positive* affective processes (seeking, care, play, and lust) and three *protective* processes (fear, rage, and panic). These seven affective domains are triggered between our limbic system and the primary functions on the right side of the brain. (We'll discuss the parts of the brain in detail in the next chapter.) These are unconscious processes, neither driven nor altered by words, and they guide us throughout our lives.

If you and I were talking and I suddenly pulled a snake from my inside jacket pocket, you would probably have an automatic fear response to it. That fear might be so great that it verges on panic, or that fear may be low and balanced by curiosity. Only someone with experience with snakes would feel only excitement. And no matter what prior dealing you've had with snakes, you would not have to consciously process your reaction. You would not think, "That's a snake. Should I run? Should I get closer?" Your reaction would be instantaneous and only secondarily word-based. You would recoil or lean in automatically.

All mammals have a fear response to snakes. Horses want to stomp them, dogs want to grab them and shake them to death. They don't know why; it just happens. But it drives behavior without conscious, sequential thought.

That's what the affective states are. They represent nonverbal, preconscious processing in your brain. You can explain these feelings and reactions, but only after the fact, by assessing the experience. Even in the moment, you need to try to identify the feeling and decide how to proceed. And we often will deny, even to ourselves, that we experience these feelings and urges. We are reluctant to admit what drives us—if we even recognize it.

All of these drive relationships. Indeed, Panksepp asserts, all of them but lust shape the core personality. (Lust does not kick in until after the core personality has been formed.)

Seeking is universal. We're all curious, and we are energized by new experiences. No one has to teach a puppy or a young chimp or a toddler to try to leave its playpen. They want to, and the urge cannot be dulled; it can only be facilitated or frustrated. Exploring is self-reinforcing through chemical processes in the brain that reward us for discovering new things. (This is also why we love to shop.) If you've ever felt "in the zone" in an activity, such as work or a hobby, that's the seeking urge. This desire to engage with the world also drives us to seek love, support, and comfort from others.

Care, in Panksepp's context, is not about priorities, but about our natural capacity and desire to care for others, especially the young. More than anything else, care builds resilience in children. This is why nature takes care very seriously. Giving and receiving care triggers opioid activity in the brain. "Pregnancy brain," also called "baby fog," is the result of the brain downplaying certain processes in order to prepare the mother to focus on her helpless infant. The effect can be contagious. Men who have been around pregnant women and mothers will have more oxytocin (sometimes called "the love hormone," discussed in chapter 3) and estrogen in their systems and less testosterone. The care urge also makes us want to cuddle baby animals or help someone in need, perhaps even a stranger.

Play is not frivolous. It is as crucial to development as it is fun. Play is the process through which children learn about behavioral limits and empathy, the foundations of socialization skills. Evidence is mounting that play and movement are critical to analytical thinking and academic performance, as well. As Catherine Tamis-LeMonda, a professor of applied psychology at New York University, recently told *The New York Times*, "We think that all domains of development are informed by children engaging in play."

Lust is driven by testosterone in both males and females.

And contrary to common belief, testosterone does not stir aggression but rather heightens desire, possibly to the point of resorting to coercion or violence to obtain the object of that desire. Because lust emerges later in life, its manifestation is influenced by personality and environment. Sex is genetic, but gender is psychobiological and therefore is far more flexible in its manifestation. Among all mammals, only humans are known to exercise conscious choice in mating.

The *fear* response is inherited, hardwired, and cross-cultural. There are many things, besides snakes, that frighten nearly all humans: darkness, enclosed spaces, heights, spiders—though, of course, we can learn to fear things, too. At a low level, fear freezes and focuses us. What was that sound? Is something moving over there? How will I get out of this crowded plane if something goes wrong? At high levels, fear compels us to flee.

Fear is different from *panic*. Panksepp describes panic as the response to feeling alone, unloved, and possibly unlovable. Babies and children may cry out of a sense of panic over not knowing where Mom is. Adults may or may not cry over separation or isolation but will feel grief.

We typically use the word *rage* to refer to an extreme verbal or physical outburst, but to Panksepp, rage is no less powerful when it's quiet. When an attachment wish is not met, it can evoke rage. We wish to flee or to fight, but we can't do either. We all get frustrated when our plans are thwarted or when people let us down. Recently the seventeen-year-old who lives in my house got mad at the twenty-two-year-old who lives in my house because the twenty-two-year-old had been wearing some of the seventeen-year-old's clothes. The younger one found the older one's favorite socks, took scissors to them, and posted video of the act on Instagram. When they brought this dispute to my attention, I told the seventeen-year-old she could have handled it better, but it was an interesting way to express her rage over being denied the respect she seeks from her older sibling.

We carry all of these within us. They drive us into and influence relational behaviors. The positive processes compel us to enter into and navigate relationships, and the protective processes kick in when relationships are threatened or lost. Relationships are fundamental to all mammals, and especially critical for humans. Relationships shaped and define us as a species.

Parenting

The evolution of parenting in the animal kingdom is not well understood, but from the sheer breadth and depth of examples it clearly gave mammals an advantage. Unlike reptiles, which are born with the instincts they will need to survive, mammals need to learn a variety of skills from one or both of their parents. The most important of these skills is the ability to interact with others of their kind, to be social. There are some mammals that live largely solitary lives, like male tigers and bears, but even they are raised by devoted mothers whose care is crucial to their brain development.

Lions, bears, and many other mammals mate for minutes. The males in those species have little to no involvement with their offspring. Males are most involved in raising their young in the relatively few species that mate for life, like wolves and humans. But humans took this strategy farther than any other species with alloparenting, or caring for others' offspring.

There are tremendous advantages to intensive parenting. It requires not just exclusive pair bonding but also a cooperative group environment that will support, and not try to break up, the relationship. This community is important. We have evolved to thrive when more adults than just our parents participate in raising us. In early human communities, group care-giving was necessary. We have a relatively short incubation period and, compared to other mammals, are born more helpless. You've probably seen images of colts and calves wobbling around, learning to walk shortly after birth. Human infants need months just to start crawling, and many years to learn how to navigate relationships with others.

"Across hunter-gatherer societies, children receive support not only from their parent, but also their siblings, grandparents, extended kin and unrelated individuals," writes evolutionary psychology researcher David M. Buss in *The Handbook of Evolutionary Psychology*. "We suggest that human social structure, characterized by lifelong, cooperative bonds that exist within and between groups, may have evolved, in part, to support the needs of human family."

In most mammal species, the life expectancy of a female does not greatly exceed her fertile years. Humans are very different and always have been, despite what you may have heard. In generations and centuries past, more people died under the age of twenty than we see today; many of them were women who did not survive childbirth. But it was not at all uncommon for some people to live to be sixty, even many thousands of years ago. Why would nature grant humans the ability to live well past their reproductive period?

Grandmothers may have been humanity's most potent advantage.

"Socially skilled and well-connected older mothers and grandmothers may have been especially valuable teachers of social and political wisdom, with associated reproductive benefits," writes Buss. "Grandmothers have been shown to positively affect outcomes, such as the survivorship and growth of their grandchildren in a number of populations."

More recent research suggests grandmothers' involvement did more than help babies survive. NPR recently reported on emerging evidence of grandmothers' role in the evolution of humans' ability to connect with each other, and to reap the associated benefits of relationships. In research among modern hunter-gatherer communities in Tanzania, anthropologist Kristen Hawkes found that mothers and grandmothers provide far more food for children than the adult male hunters, who rarely return with a kill. Primatologist Sarah Hrdy argues that the alloparenting necessary to care for offspring with the prolonged state of helplessness of human babies laid the groundwork for our advanced social skills.

"People often try to explain the fact that humans are so good at cooperating by saying, well, we needed to cooperate in order to succeed at big game hunting, or so that men in one group could bond with other men to go wipe out the neighboring group," Hrdy said. "What that doesn't do is explain why these traits emerge so early." Babies' abilities to engage with others are surprisingly sophisticated, as we'll discuss more in chapter 3.

As a species and as individuals, relationships shape us, at least as much as and perhaps more than genetics. For better or for worse.

Friend or Foe? The Safety Ethic

A few years ago, I decided to adopt two dogs. When I visited the breeder, I sat down on the floor to see which pups from the litter would approach me first. One came bounding toward me, overjoyed to see a person. She was the first pick—she was clearly already attuned to people. Two other puppies ignored me and kept playing. Another watched me from under a table for a minute or so, then slowly ambled over. Once she was sure I was safe, she stayed with me, and she became my second choice.

Even at ten weeks, these dogs perceived new situations differently. Two were indifferent to people (at least to me), one was very excited, and the fourth was somewhere in the middle. In the two I took home, those temperaments have remained consistent. The second dog I chose is still a little wary of people, is quicker to bark (especially at anyone wearing a hat), and will look for opportunities to get affection from me when her older, bolder sister is not putting herself front and center.

Neuroception is the unconscious, right-brain process that tells us whether it's safe to engage in social behavior, or whether we might be in danger. Three of the twelve cranial nerves, which carry information between the brain and body, tell our bodies either to prepare to flee or fight, or to relax and enjoy interacting with others. And because those nerves are involved, our faces—especially our eyes and cheeks—will provide strong indications of our neuroceptive states.

Just like my dogs, people have varying neuroceptive default settings. But toxic stress and trauma can reset a person's neuroception so that he or she becomes much more likely to perceive a neutral situation as threatening. A combat veteran may have a more powerful response to the sound of a car backfiring than someone who has not experienced war.

Most veterans can learn to return to their prewar default settings. Toxic stress, however, is different. Toxic stress changes the trajectory of the developmental process of perceiving situations.

Narvaez's work indicates that people with neuroceptive challenges respond to life events and stress triggers differently. She asserts that the mindset becomes protective, and that this shapes or reshapes personality traits, manufacturing what she calls the safety ethic.

Safety ethic sounds positive, like a company boasting about its low rate of workplace injuries. But in our context, safety ethic prioritizes personal safety above all else, all the time. This leads to looking for, and often seeing, threats everywhere. This is a constant distraction, hindering learning and the very social interactions that children need to engage in, in order to learn how to feel safe among people they don't know.

If you see anger and rage, as Panksepp does, as a stuck fight-flight response, you can see how the safety ethic leads to a propensity for aggression. A person with a strong safety ethic will be more likely to view a person of a different race as a threat, or to respond to an accidental bump in a crowded store as a precursor to an attack.

Safety ethic also compels people to seek groups that share their perceptions of danger. And within a group organized for safety, there will be a hierarchy that the members need to navigate. In nature, we generally see more hierarchy among predators, such as wolves and hyenas, who organize in order to hunt. Chimpanzees, who are omnivores, organize to hunt and to fight rival chimp groups.

In the early 1970s, renowned primate researcher Jane Goodall and her team chronicled a four-year war between previously united chimp communities in Gombe Stream National Park in Tanzania. This year, researchers working with Goodall's extensive data sets announced that they'd determined the primary cause of the war: a power struggle. "The degree of subgrouping in grooming and association networks increased sharply in 1971 and 1972, a period characterized by a dominance struggle between three high-ranking males and unusually high male:female sex ratios."

For humans within a safety ethic group, one's in-group status is more important than a larger worldview. What people in other groups are doing is of little concern, unless that group is perceived to be a threat. There is often a focus on geography and protecting territory, as we see in everything from street gangs to nations. All of this limits the development of empathy. Narvaez asserts that the safety ethic limits imagination, encourages narcissism, and leads to burnout or exhaustion.

Narvaez also says that safety ethic drives the stories that we tell each other, reinforcing our positions within the group and justifying the group's belief about other groups (in other words, myths). These narratives are often long on rigid morality and short on empathy for anyone outside the group. And because language is the primary tool that shapes culture, a narrative of self-protection can grow into a culture of self-protection that is handed down through generations. The problem is that humans evolved to live in a much different way than the vast majority of us live today, and we're not good at turning away from a safety ethic, even when it's no longer needed.

Civilization Changed Everything, But Not All for the Better

When was the last time you marveled at the stars? Even if you happened to think about this and went outside at night, you probably wouldn't see more than a scattering of a few dozen of the brightest ones. In his 2013 book *The End of Night: Searching for Natural Darkness in an Age of Artificial Light*, Paul Bogard argues that we are rapidly losing something fundamental to our identity in the name of progress.

"Since the beginning of time, a sky plush with stars was part of the common human experience," he wrote in *National Geographic*. "Everywhere on Earth, on most nights, our ancestors came face to face with the universe. This experience influenced their religious beliefs, mythologies, art—their very understanding of their place in creation. Today, because of light pollution, two-thirds of those in the United States and western Europe live where they cannot see the Milky Way, and 99 percent of us live under skies polluted by light. . . . Most Americans under 40 have never known real darkness. All over the globe our nights are growing brighter, and almost nowhere are they growing darker."

We've rushed into this situation with almost no regard for the consequences. In addition to the effects of burning fossil fuels to support our illumination addiction, Borgard notes, "studies increasingly link our overuse of light at night with health concerns such as sleep disorders, diabetes, obesity, and cancer." And that's probably just scratching the surface.

We also live with auditory stimulation that our ancestors

would have found alarming. A research project called One Square Inch of Silence, which studies "soundscape management" in Olympic National Park in Washington, defines a naturally quiet place as one where you might hear no man-made sounds for up to 15 minutes. The researchers estimate that there are fewer than ten such sites left in the U.S.

Worldwide light and noise pollution are just two examples of the ways in which we've deviated dramatically from the evolutionary path we followed for most of our history.

Homo sapiens have been around for about 200,000 years, and we spent the first 190,000 or so as hunter-gatherers. The life was relatively simple. Most would have met few humans outside their own tribes, which tended not to travel very far, and whatever strangers they did see would have looked a lot like them. They spent a few hours a day looking for food and might relocate a couple of times a year with the seasons in order to follow their food sources. Most of the time, it was a good life. That is the scenario in which our brains evolved.

Then around 10,000 years ago, we began to transition to farming, settling in one place, living among much greater numbers of fellow humans, and calling ourselves nations—in other words, establishing civilizations. This change took around 4,000 years, according to James Scott, author of *Against the Grain: A Deep History of the Earliest States*. People resisted.

In 2017, Scott told Vox.com:

> The idea that hunters and gatherers and foragers were living hand to mouth and one day away from starvation is nonsense, even for those in pretty marginal areas where there is less access to natural migrations of fish and animals

> and the fruiting seasons of trees and so on. The truth is that staying in one place, which is what civilization more or less forced us to do, wasn't all that healthy for us, and our human ancestors resisted [it] strongly for a very long time.
>
> Hunter-gatherers' skeletons [found in modern times] are much larger because they had fewer interruptions in growth, and their bones show almost no signs of malnutrition, whereas the people in the agricultural civilizations are both shorter and their bones and teeth are less robust. It's clear that people outside these grain civilizations were healthier than the people inside.
>
> Hunters and gatherers only spent half of their time working, and the rest was spent in play or leisure. By contrast, those early agrarian civilizations involved much more labor and drudgery. [They] also involved a narrower diet that turned out mostly carbohydrates. And that's why people resisted this transition, and why many had to be forced into this change. The first civilizations were very hard and unhealthy places that gave us most of our first infectious diseases, many of which are still with us. They also produced the first coercive states that took slaves and oppressed large numbers of people.
>
> It's really only in the last 200 years or so that we've enjoyed the health and longevity that we do today. But this initial period when we think civilization was created was, in fact, a really dark period for humanity.

And in evolutionary terms, it's a blip. Our brains haven't had much time to adjust to all of this, including meeting people who look, act, speak, and think much differently from ourselves. Our brains categorize everything instantly, even before we're conscious of it, and our highly effective warning systems were developed when the greatest threats were large predatory mammals. When faced with other humans with dramatically different skin tones or features, the brain's automatic response is to categorize it as "other" and, possibly, "threat."

As Scott notes, agriculture also exposed us to new diseases. But our brains are not new to illness, and disgust and nausea are defense mechanisms. When we see or hear someone vomiting, or smell vomit, we often have a strong urge to vomit, too. This is an old instinct from when we all ate the same food. If your friend has a bad reaction to the berries, it's a good idea to purge them from your own system as well. Or if the illness isn't food-related, we want to stay away from the person with symptoms to avoid catching the same thing. A recent study out of Stockholm University found that experiment participants, about eight times out of ten, were able to identify the "after" photo in before-and-after images showing just the faces of people who had been injected with a mild irritant to provoke flu-like symptoms.

We have a natural proclivity to find things disgusting. There are personal variations—you may be grossed out by things that don't particularly bother me and vice versa—but we're all prone to find certain sights, smells, and even sounds revolting. Unfortunately, we also are prone to develop repulsions based on less tangible stimuli as well as assumptions about other people's habits, motives, and willingness to hurt us. This is how we fall into "us vs. them" thinking.

When you are around "them," you have a cortisol process. Then when you remove yourself, you relax, which feels like a reward and reinforces your identification and avoidance of "them" because it literally feels better. But for some people, that's not the only dynamic at work. Some will want to confront "them," verbally or violently, in order to trigger an adrenaline rush and testosterone boost. Fighting can feel good.

People living in an unsafe environment develop an aggressiveness about keeping the group safe—the safety ethic. Like chimps, they establish hierarchies in order to fight more effectively. Safety becomes the first developmental task, the first need, prioritized above all others, and everyone in the group is responsible for it.

Hierarchies are not hardwired into us. When animals establish a pecking order or some relational process that determines role, they do so for safety. They are going to hunt, attack, or defend. In a pack of dogs, the strongest and most fierce takes the middle position, flanked by the next strongest, and so on, so that the weakest and oldest are last to join the aggression.

The history behind Thanksgiving illustrates the ways humans organize around principles of trust and sharing, or around a safety ethic.

Native Americans in what are now the Mid-Atlantic states lived amid plenty when the pilgrims arrived. Clams literally popped out of the sand when they walked on the beach, and lobsters could be caught just by wading into the water. No one went hungry, and there was little conflict between neighboring tribes.

The pilgrims' lives could not have been more different. They had fled a society in which they had felt persecuted in a part of the world where ownership and status mattered, where groups lived in clearly delineated spaces and sometimes went to war over access to resources or simply over their beliefs. Upon arriving in the New World, the first things they built were a center hall and a place to store their cannons. They also assigned ranks and roles to everyone in their community and practiced for war.

When the Native Americans engaged with the pilgrims, they tried to make it clear that the pilgrims could choose whether the two could live without conflict. They did not seek to dominate the pilgrims for their own safety because they were not grounded in an historical safety ethic. The pilgrims, in contrast, were highly safety-minded. So were most of the Old Worlders who followed, and because of this, most of the Native Americans were slowly but methodically wiped out.

When we build communities on the foundation of a safety ethic, it gives us permission to violate those we perceive as others and rationalizes any behavior that protects the group. When we operate out of a safety ethic, because of the chronic toxic stress that we've experienced in our lives, it denigrates our capacity to operate morally. Cultures of competition are driven by cortisol, the body's primary stress hormone. It's the fuel that drives competition and the safety ethic.

History proves that we can be quite comfortable looking at everyone as either allies or enemies. To some extent, we are hardwired for this sort of outlook; at the very least, it feels normal under certain circumstances. And there are times when it's unavoidable. We could not have stopped the Axis powers in the 1940s with efforts to build community. But fighting that war took a toll, even on the victors. The Cold War that followed is an excellent example of how the safety ethic can become a cultural value that is passed down from generation to generation. And after the collapse of the Soviet Union, many transitioned easily into fearing and hating Islamist terror groups, and perhaps all Muslims. Not without reason, of course, but we've barely acknowledged, much less grappled with, the long-term costs.

Opposing the safety ethic is not easy. Think about what happens to people who challenge cultural values. These are implicit emotions, hard to define, like my World War II veteran father's love of the American flag, which he taught to me. It would be easy for me to get angry at people who seem to disrespect the flag; I have to stop myself and think through whether that's really the person's intent.

We have to consciously think about enlarging our groups, or as I sometimes call it, building the "we." But first we need to come to terms with the role that stress plays in tearing us apart. Families that experience generations of toxic stress will teach the safety ethic, and communities will coalesce around it. It's protective and adaptive, so we can't teach it away. We have to address, in as many people as we can, the underlying toxic stress-inducing experiences and events that afflict so many early in their lives.

CHAPTER 2

Stress, the Body, and the Brain

"Rabbits live close to death and when death comes closer than usual, thinking about survival leaves little room for anything else."

—from *Watership Down* by Richard Adams

Driving home from work one evening about ten years ago, I noticed a light in my bedroom window. I quietly chastised myself for leaving the light on but didn't think any more of it until I entered the kitchen door and found food and dishes strewn across the floor. In that moment, I realized that my home had been burglarized.

The house was silent, and I quickly concluded that the intruder had long since fled. Still, as I walked from room to room, trying to determine what was missing, my body shook, and I struggled to think clearly. I called the police, and by the time they arrived, about a half-hour later, I was relatively calm, and they guided me through the reporting process.

But for the next day or two I still felt activated. I wanted to *do* something, so I called my credit card companies, found out where my cards had been used since the theft, and visited those places to ask for images from their surveillance cameras. I took those images to the police, and the thieves were arrested.

For a long time after, however, every time I drove home I grew tense, and I looked to see if that bedroom light was on. As a therapist, I knew what to do. Every night for a week, I turned the light on, then went out and drove around the block twenty times. After I did that, my body relaxed. But to this day, if the light in the sky and the weather are similar to how they were the night of the break-in, I look for the light, and I feel a slight twinge of fear. Our bodies don't forget.

I told that story once in a seminar, and a member of the audience raised her hand to tell me that she'd also recently experienced a home break-in, and that my story had triggered a stress response in her. I told her to breathe slowly, not deeply, and focus on exhaling. I suggested that she leave the room and asked someone who knew her to go with her and give her a hug. She was able to return later, but the incident illustrated for everyone, including me, just how powerful a hold stress can have on us. Stress affects us physically, cognitively, and emotionally. The more intense and sustained the stress, the more severe and long-lasting its impact.

Trauma and Stress

It's important to distinguish between toxic stress and trauma. They can be related, but trauma is, by definition, intolerable. The mind will look for ways to compensate for the pain of a traumatic event, and brain function can be altered, as we'll discuss soon.

The response to trauma is most notably different from stress in terms of recollection. We're all familiar with the way most memories degrade over time. Some things slip away altogether, and other things become hazier and harder to recall. A traumatic event, however, can be seared into your memory in excruciating detail for the rest of your life. This is because of the way the brain is activated at that moment. That is a core component of a traumatic experience, and how one deals with that, and how much relational support one has, determine whether post-traumatic stress will follow.

Toxic stress may not have any flashbulb, incidental memories attached to it. Memories of stress resulting from neglect, abuse, poverty, and other toxic stressors we've identified may become less vivid later in life if circumstances change and relational capacities improve.

There are three levels of stress: positive, tolerable, and toxic.

Positive stress is moderate, short-lived, and essential to healthy development. We all experience varying levels of it throughout the day, and it drives performance. It gets us going in the morning; it gives us a list of things to do; it assigns priorities and helps us to engage in behavior that's important to survival and development. Making new friends, starting daycare or preschool, welcoming a new baby sibling into the family—these are all typical stressors children face that, under the right circumstances, are beneficial to development.

Tolerable stress is deeper and longer-lasting, the kind often associated with sudden or impending loss—death, illness, accidents, divorce, unemployment. Most of us are fortunate enough to have family, friends, and colleagues we can turn to for support. Just knowing that someone is there to care for us, hug us, and listen to us, helps us get through the darkest days following the event and sets us on a course to recover and to function normally, despite memories of the loss.

Toxic stress is stress that results from two sets of conditions: a) a severe, ongoing situation like abuse (physical, emotional, or sexual); neglect (physical or emotional); household dysfunction (substance abuse, mental illness, divorce, abuse of mother) or combinations of such circumstances; and b), a lack of relationships that could provide support for the sufferer.

After experiencing positive and tolerable stress, a person can return to baseline. After toxic stress, the baseline is changed. Toxic stress changes the way the brain functions—not just psychologically but biologically, at the level we often refer to as "hardwiring"—and those changes may be permanent without intervention.

During and long after periods of toxic stress, the stress responses are activated more frequently and for longer periods than normal or necessary. The stress response will engage at lower thresholds to events that might not be stressful to others. And because the brain and body are so deeply, inextricably connected and reliant on each other, the effects are wide-ranging and profound. Without support, children who experience toxic stress are set up for developmental, neurobiological, health, and relational problems.

The Adverse Childhood Experiences (ACEs) study, organized by the Centers for Disease Control and Kaiser Permanente, has been tracking young participants into adulthood, collecting data about their health, since the late 1990s. The findings have been staggering. In 2006, a report published in the *Journal of Integral Theory and Practice* noted that "research . . . strongly implicates childhood traumas, or 'adverse childhood experiences,' in the *ten leading causes of death in the United States*" (emphasis in the original).

The report continues: "History may well show that the discovery of the impact of ACEs on noninfectious causes of death was as powerful and revolutionary an insight as Pasteur's once controversial theory that germs cause infectious disease. His ideas were slow to be adopted, but are now universally accepted. Similarly, ACEs parallel what Pasteur offered—an underlying syndrome implicated in noninfectious causes of death. This is truly a remarkable discovery that is likely to change the way in which the field of medicine is viewed and practiced."

Put simply, adverse childhood experiences disrupt the child's neurodevelopment, which leads to social and emotional cognitive impairment. These in turn can lead to the adoption of health-risk behaviors that can result in disease, disability, social problems, and even early death. To understand why, you need to understand some of the fundamentals of how mammals, including humans, have evolved to respond to stress and the impact it has on how the brain develops and functions.

Mammalian Brain Development

Like all mammal brains, human brains develop from the bottom up, starting with the most primitive survival functions and working up to complex, higher-order functions that drive goal-oriented behavior. At birth, only about 25 percent of the brain is developed, leaving the rest dependent on early life experiences. Only the lower regions of the brain, known as the hindbrain, are fully functional at birth.

In the hindbrain, the cerebellum and the brainstem mediate alertness, arousal, and the physiological state of the body through the regulation of temperature, respiration, and heart rate. The brain processes linked to the hindbrain are reactive. When survival is at stake—and during actual or perceived traumatic experiences—higher brain functions, such as reasoning, go off-line as the brain prioritizes quick response ("fight or flight").

The central regions, or the midbrain, develop in response to the quantity and quality of early attachments and experiences. One of the most important areas of the midbrain is the limbic region, which regulates emotion, motivation, and goal-directed action. The limbic region also integrates memory and the engagement of attachment tendencies.

Also in the midbrain, the hippocampus organizes explicit memory and conscious learning. The hippocampus links to the medial temporal lobe, which plays a role in recalling facts and autobiographical details and identifying the context of early and ongoing experiences. The amygdala processes experiences of fear, attachment, early memory, and emotion. Finally, the thalamus connects this central region to the upper region of the brain and relays motor and sensory signals to the cerebral cortex, where complex functions occur.

The forebrain includes the cortical regions, which compare internal and external information with past experiences. This allows the prefrontal and parietal lobes to analyze situations, make decisions, and pursue goals. The orbital medial prefrontal cortex regulates attachment and social relationships and has a strong connection to the body's sensory and regulatory systems.

Finally, the cerebral cortex is the most complex region of the brain, processing perception, thinking, and reasoning. The frontal-most part of the cerebral cortex, the prefrontal cortex, is one of the last regions in the brain to become fully functional. Linked to the lower limbic system brainstem and other bodily functions, the prefrontal cortex manages thoughts and feelings, relaying related messages to the rest of the brain and the body.

The Stress Response

The brain is one part of the staggeringly complex nervous system. We will focus on those structures and processes that are most closely involved in responding to stress and returning to baseline.

The brain and spinal cord make up the central nervous system (CNS). The nerves radiating out from the spinal cord, carrying signals between the brain and all parts of the body, are known as the peripheral nervous system (PNS). Signals are carried via an array of neurotransmitters, chemicals that are able to travel across the synapses between neurons.

The PNS has two components: the somatic nervous system (voluntary movement, like raising your arm), and the autonomic nervous system (unconscious processes such as breathing, blinking, etc.). And the autonomic nervous system includes the sympathetic nervous system ("fight or flight") and the parasympathetic nervous system ("rest and digest"). This is where we'll focus.

When you are relaxed, the parasympathetic nervous system is in control. An extreme example is how you feel after Thanksgiving dinner. When you are stressed, the sympathetic nervous system takes over. It's designed to immediately redirect all your energy into action when facing a possible threat. Blood flows from core to hands, feet, and head to prepare for movement. Pupils dilate, salivation stops, and the hormones adrenaline and cortisol start flowing.

The limbic system, in the midbrain, facilitates a bottom-up reaction to fear and stress, activating the amygdala, the hippocampus, thalamus, and hypothalamus. When the limbic system is activated, the forebrain shuts down in order to focus on survival. That's why in a moment of panic, it's hard to think clearly.

Most of the time, you're not aware of what the hypothalamus is doing. It sifts through all incoming sensory data and decides what's important, requiring immediate attention, and what isn't. When you enter a room and smell something out of the ordinary, you notice it because your hypothalamus draws your attention to it. If you determine the source of the smell, or it doesn't seem to suggest any danger, your hypothalamus will stop alerting you to the stimulus and you'll "get used to it."

Think about how your shoes feel on your feet, or how your shirt sleeves feel on your arms. A few seconds ago you weren't paying any attention at all to those sensations. When you read the words, your hypothalamus directed your attention there, but until then, your hypothalamus had suppressed that type of input because it was less important than focusing on this book. The hypothalamus allows us to focus on tasks.

If the hypothalamus is like an air-traffic controller, then the amygdala is an alarm. If someone suddenly yells "Hey!", or if you notice movement in your peripheral vision, it's your amygdala that tells your body to turn and look. Then the hippocampus, the brain's librarian, tries to identify the source of the sound or movement and decides how to respond. If you see that the person who yelled "hey" was not talking to you, or that the movement was just your cat, the hippocampus tells the alarm to switch off. The hippocampus organizes memory and learning as well as regulating emotions. Most important, the hippocampus regulates the amygdala's response to a perceived threat, balancing the limbic system.

In the face of a threat, there is a cascading response. First, the hypothalamus sends precursor hormones and neurotransmitter alerts to the pituitary gland, which also releases a precursor hormone to the adrenal glands, which are located on top of the kidneys, resulting in blasts of cortisol and, if the threat is dire, adrenaline. The hypothalamus also releases cortisol into the prefrontal cortex. All of this occurs in a fraction of a second, and the message is clear and concise: Hey, do something!

There is a constant feedback loop during stress between cortisol and the neurotransmitters in the brain that react to it. This is why people who are experiencing toxic stress are constantly monitoring their surroundings and interactions. Their brains become hyperalert to potential triggers because the amygdala and the hypothalamus are working together to alert the brain and the body to potential threats. The hypothalamic–pituitary adrenal (HPA) axis stays on high alert, constantly regulating the metabolic, cardiovascular, immune, reproductive, and central nervous systems.

A malfunctioning fire alarm that frequently blares even when there is no fire creates a dangerous situation because people will begin to ignore it. Likewise, an amygdala that fires incorrectly is dangerous to emotional processing—but because the person can't ignore it. The amygdalae of children who experience neglect and abuse in the first year of their lives are 40 percent larger than average and hyper-responsive. And no matter how those children's lives may improve, or what kind of therapy they receive, their amygdalae will never shrink. They are permanently hardwired with an over-responsive alert system that is quick to react and slow to shut down. Their behavior becomes organized around fear, and they have trouble adjusting to different life situations, particularly those outside their comfort zones.

Toxic stress also decreases the density of the corpus callosum, the bundle of neurons that connect the right and left hemispheres of the brain. This makes it more difficult to coordinate the two sides and, as we'll see, this has lifelong consequences.

Two Sides to Every Story: The Right and Left Hemispheres of the Brain

You've probably heard that the right and left hemispheres of the brain have specialized roles—the right side is creative and emotional, and the left, logical and precise. This is a simplification. Many functions rely on structures on both sides. For our purposes, however, the generalizations are useful.

To see an example of how right- and left-brain processes differ but complement each other, write down the names of the streets that you travel on when driving from home to work, or vice versa. Then draw lines representing those roads and how they intersect with each other. Your map need not be precise or to scale. Now look at those lines, and mark each intersection with an "R" for a right turn or "L" for left.

The first task, naming the streets, is a left-brain process because it's word-based. The next task, drawing the lines, is almost all spatial, and therefore right brain. For the final step, marking the turns, you need both hemispheres. "Left" and "right" are words, but they only have meaning in a specific spatial context. And you might have found yourself checking your right and left hands or even imagining your hands on the wheel, making the turn, before writing down "left" or "right." It's challenging, and you probably have a fully functioning corpus callosum.

The skills housed in the right side of the brain—such as instincts and feelings that we colloquially attribute to our guts—are older, evolutionarily, than those in the left. Have you ever visited a museum and seen a painting that you just love? That seems to communicate with you? That consumes you? In that moment, if someone were to ask why you like that painting, you'd say something like, "It's beautiful. I like the colors and the images. It really speaks to me. I feel it." Notice that these are not descriptive terms.

So then imagine that you walk down the hall of the museum and see another painting, and you cannot stand it. You have a visceral reaction to it and wonder if the painter was mentally disturbed. And in this case, too, you might struggle to put the feeling into words. "This is the ugliest thing I've ever seen. I don't want to look at it. I don't like the way it makes me feel."

Whether related to art or to anything else, you've probably encountered difficulty in trying to convey an emotion. The Dictionary of Obscure Sorrows is a Web site dedicated to naming and describing emotional hues and shades far outside the primary colors of happiness, sadness, anger, etc., and the descriptions can be rather poetic in their attempts to pin down the ephemeral. The reason for this is grounded in biology: Emotions reside in the right side of the brain, which does not use language. Only when the information moves over to the left brain, through the corpus callosum, can we begin to express these feelings in words. But you lose some of the emotional intensity and valence.

The right brain drives our emotional capacity. Affect, the experience of emotion, is a right-brain process, and so your affective state, the one that you live with and deal with and that drives your emotional processes, is a right-brain experience. The right brain is responsible for sadness and depression but also bonding and connection. It processes intimate gestures such as facial expressions and gaze directions as well as tone of voice and touch, and it's through such nonverbal cues that we gain our earliest understandings of the world.

The right side is also where shame and regret live. We've all had the experience of remembering things we did long ago that still cause us embarrassment or feelings of remorse. These nagging feelings are supposed to help prevent you from repeating mistakes.

The left hemisphere of the brain is the processing center, and accordingly, it's where language originates. Broca's area, in the left frontal lobe, helps us produce coherent speech. Wernicke's area, in the left temporal lobe, processes the speech of others.

These are relatively recent additions, appearing in humans about one hundred thousand years ago. They link to the larynx, but they reside in the left hemisphere.

Around forty thousand years ago, our brains began to change in ways that are not well understood, but the results were dramatic. Our language became much more sophisticated, and we started to create art and take care of the dead, suggesting belief in an afterlife. These indicate a leap in our level of self-awareness and intentionality. There is self-talk in these acts: "I'm going to make markings on the wall, and the others will like it." Or, "I will prepare my mother's body for her journey to the unseen place." And to have that type of awareness, you need verbalization processes.

The prefrontal cortex—the foremost areas of the right and left hemispheres, just behind the forehead—is where "you" exist. The size and placement of the prefrontal cortex is what makes humans unique among mammals.

While each hemisphere has its own talents, it's not uncommon for one side to attempt to compensate for shortcomings in the other. In extreme cases, one side will shut the other down. As Daniel Siegel, professor of psychiatry at UCLA and founder of the Mindful Awareness Research Center, puts it, "the two [sides] working together as a functional whole is the best way to go . . . unless it is better that you not feel what your body is telling you or that you should not understand logically what is happening around you." These are human survival instincts kicking in, helping one to cope with difficult life experiences.

Even levels of stress that most of us would consider common can affect brain functions. In 2014, a *Washington Post* reporter tried to figure out why loving, caring parents with no mental deficiencies can forget about a child in a car seat, sometimes for hours, sometimes with tragic results. David Diamond, a professor of molecular physiology at the University of South Florida, explained that in certain circumstances the basal ganglia, the brain's autopilot for routine tasks, can take over, without us even noticing.

"The important factors that keep showing up involve a combination of stress, emotion, lack of sleep and change in routine, where the basal ganglia is trying to do what it's supposed to do, and the conscious mind is too weakened to resist," Diamond explained. "What happens is that the memory circuits in a vulnerable hippocampus literally get overwritten, like with a computer program. Unless the memory circuit is rebooted—such as if the child cries, or, you know, if the wife mentions the child in the back—it can entirely disappear."

When children experience toxic stress, the brain copes the only way it knows how: by activating the primitive survival structures (limbic, hindbrain, and bodily processes). Such activation in turn triggers the stress response system and essentially shuts down the left brain—perhaps with the intent, Siegel suggests, to protect one from logically understanding the distress.

Stress and Memory

My earliest memory is of a picnic with my twin sister and some family friends. We were having fun, listening to the radio, when suddenly the adults' moods changed, and we had to pack up and go home. Only much later did I understand why. It was November 22, 1963. I was just three years old, so I didn't know who President Kennedy was and had never heard the word "assassination." But I still carry this photo-like memory of that day in my brain, and I can communicate it verbally because I have easy access to it. It's my twin sister's first memory, as well, because our ability to form explicit memories—recollections of events and experiences—were coming online at about the same time.

When is the last time you rode a bike? For some it will be years, perhaps decades. And yet if asked you'd probably say that yes, of course you know how to ride a bike. And you probably could. Same with swimming. If you hadn't gone swimming in years, then fell into water, you wouldn't start deconstructing the mechanics of swimming in your head. You'd just do it. You don't think about walking down stairs, and if you did suddenly pay close attention to all the movements, you'd increase your chances of falling. A skill is an implicit memory, and implicit memory processes are never lost.

Explicit memories, however, are subject to expiration. Can you recall what you ate for breakfast on this date three months ago? Probably not. A lot of inconsequential information gets written over, and if you search for a particular memory, you may not find it. In fact, your left brain has a trick for dealing with gaps in memory: It makes stuff up. The term for this is *confabulation.*

Think about your last argument with your significant other. You don't know what they said, and you're banking on them not remembering what either of you said. And you started constructing memories so you can enter some sort of negotiation over what might have happened. Your left brain is incapable of remembering the exact context of conversations or precise sequences of events. It starts with what it can recall, then builds a logical narrative between those points. In this process, coherence matters more than accuracy. This is why eyewitness testimony can be so unreliable.

The right brain, however, forgets very little, if anything. That's why we rely so heavily on intuition. The problem is that the right brain can't tell what's real and what's not real. It can imagine things, and that process can be so strong that it can change the way the left brain works.

Think about watching a scary movie in a theater. You know exactly where you are, and you know that you are watching two-dimensional moving images projected onto a screen. But you can still experience an adrenaline rush that startles you and causes you to jump in your seat. Now think about walking back to your car after the movie. Do you feel the urge to check the back seat or the trunk? When you get home, are you inspecting the closets and peeking behind the shower curtain? All of this is the right brain imposing its will on the left brain and the body.

This is how toxic stress builds propensities for behavior, responding to real, perceived, and imagined threats. Over time, the right brain becomes dominant, driving behaviors in such a way that the person follows hunches and acts on feelings.

Your body doesn't produce a lot of adrenaline. After an hour of an adrenaline rush, your body is exhausted, and your adrenaline store is depleted. But cortisol is different. Your body can keep producing it, if that's what your environment demands. It delivers energy to your body by breaking down sugars very quickly but inefficiently. It will then resort to breaking down proteins, which are stored in muscles, organs, cell walls, and immune system components like T-cells. Cortisol can damage all of them. People with generalized anxiety disorders have higher risk for organistic cancers and twice the risk for early death.

But how can experiences early in life have such long-term consequences? To answer that, we need to start in infancy.

CHAPTER 3

Home Is Where the Start Is

"I feel sorry for little babies . . . When a little baby is born into this cold world, he's confused! He's frightened! He needs something to cheer him up. . . . The way I see it, as soon as a baby is born, he should be issued a banjo!"

—Linus, "Peanuts", 1960

There is a scene in season two of *This Is Us*, the hit family drama on NBC, that stands out for both its sweetness and its wisdom. The smart, big-hearted, but tightly wound Randall is stressing out over the impending arrival of his first child and in a moment of vulnerability unburdens himself to a hardware store clerk. A father himself, the man smiles and assures Randall, "Babies come with the answers. They come out, they look up at you, they tell you who you are. Tomorrow, you'll have all the answers you need."

To say that newborns come with answers is an oversimplification, of course, but they are amazingly adept at engaging, bewitching and, in a manner of speaking, training the adults on whom they rely. A study published in 2017 in the *Proceedings of the National Academy of Sciences* reported that when infants and adults stare at each other intently, their brain waves sync. One of the lead researchers, Victoria Leong, a psychologist at the University of Cambridge, told the *Washington Post* that the findings are "giving new insights into infants' amazing abilities to connect to, and tune in with, their adult caregivers."

Also in 2017, the Princeton University Baby Lab reported that the timbre of adults' baby talk is remarkably similar across many disparate languages, including Spanish, Russian, and Cantonese. The researchers wrote, "Shifts in timbre between adult-directed and infant-directed speech may represent a universal form of communication that mothers implicitly use to engage their babies and support their language learning." (The study focused on mothers, but the team suspected that similar results would be found among fathers.) This research is outside my areas of expertise, but I can't help but wonder if the explanation is that babies teach their doting parents by responding most eagerly to the tones they hear (or like) best.

These bonding processes start well before birth with oxytocin, a hormone that also acts as a neurotransmitter. Oxytocin plays a key role in all forms of bonding and social behavior, but the most important is focusing the attention of new parents. If you're a mother, it's likely that when you first held your child, you felt like you could never love another thing as much as you loved that baby in that moment. That's an oxytocin high. Oxytocin drives pair bonding and maternal-child attachment; it engenders trust and caring. Giving birth brings on a tsunami of oxytocin to offset the stress hormones of the previous nine months and to compel the mother to focus all her attention on her helpless child.

Not surprisingly, the highest levels of oxytocin are found in mothers. The next highest are found in women who have been around mothers, then men who have been around mothers. The lowest levels are in men who don't spend any time around mothers. Caring is a neurochemical process that nature has entrusted to maternal caregivers. That doesn't mean it can't be learned by children who are not raised by their mothers. That's just the easiest method.

Mothers are also awash in endogenous (naturally occurring) opioids. At the molecular level, endogenous opioids are no different from pharmaceutical opioids—which is precisely why the latter are so addicting (as we'll discuss later). Play and caring load our brains with endogenous opioids, and we keep seeking that rush. We co-regulate (balance) these levels with the people we love, and that's why we miss them when they aren't around: because our levels of endogenous opioids drop and we experience something like withdrawal.

The attachment process is hardwired in us and provides the commodity for emotional exchange for the rest of our lives. When it's undermined in the first year of life, it takes a lot longer to repair it later on. This is true in all mammals, which is why nature has gone to such lengths to ensure that mammal parents, or at least mothers, are deeply invested in their offspring's development.

Communication Loops, Joy, and Shame

Newborns tend to have one style of crying—the full-on wail. Gas pains, hunger, cold, whatever the unpleasant stimulus, they just let loose with a cry that insists, "I don't like this! Fix it!" After around two months, most children start to develop a proximity cry, which is more aligned with the severity of the discomfort. If something is just bothering an infant, as opposed to hurting her, she can whimper a little, then wait and listen for someone approaching. If she hears someone nearby, she is less apt to cry again or increase the intensity of the crying. She feels confident that those hands from heaven are coming, and she will be made comfortable or entertained and life will be good again. This is a baby's first step in learning to communicate.

Siegel proposes that emotional communication is an important component of how interpersonal relationships shape the emotional and social development of the mind. Attachment is formed through the communication that occurs between the right brain of a baby and the right brain of a caregiver. For the baby, that relationship becomes the foundation for all relationship-building skills throughout life.

At the same time the baby is testing out proximity crying, her body and brain are learning to regulate cortisol, the major stress hormone. Cortisol regulation processes continue throughout infancy but really kick off at two months. Children who do not weather the cortisol storm well will have increased risk for emotional and social challenges when they go off to school, and the heightened risk can continue all the way through high school. (The research ends at that point, but there is no reason to think those problems would not carry on into adulthood.) Cortisol regulation begins with co-regulation between infant and caregiver within the attachment process.

Hormones and neurotransmitters also help ensure that 95 percent of parent-infant interactions are positive. Babies are fun! In the earliest months their smiles are mostly related to gas, but even the parents who know this don't care; babies' smiles are like gifts. Think of a three-month-old lifting his head to look around for the first time, or a ten-month-old letting go of the coffee table and taking her first tentative steps, seeing the happiness and encouragement these acts elicit from adults. With each milestone like this, the child's capacity for play expands, building the brain's joy processes. This feedback loop of joy strengthens the bonds between baby and caregiver. Neuropsychologist Dr. Allan Schore asserts that our capacity for joy is developed in the first year of life.

Then around eighteen months and into the so-called "terrible twos," everything changes. This is when most babies are exploring and experimenting relentlessly, often breaking things, putting themselves in danger, and making a general nuisance of themselves. Parents suddenly find themselves constantly saying "No!" and steering their toddler away from enticements such as stairs, power outlets, and the dog's tail. This is how shame processes are formed, slowly, one small interaction at a time.

We generally think of shame as entirely negative, but it serves an important developmental purpose. Shame is different from guilt. Guilt is related to expectations and plans, which are inherently word-based ("I did something wrong, and I know I shouldn't have done it") and therefore resides in the left prefrontal cortex. Shame is more implicit, or instinctive. It can be related to expectations, but it's rooted in our relationships with others and how they see us. Shame is a deeper emotion than guilt, so deep that we can feel it in our bodies. We feel worthless; not just unloved, but unlovable. But like joy, it plays an important role in our relationships throughout our lives. Because we feel shame, we learn the boundaries of relationships and figure out the rules that make relationships safe. We loathe

the feeling of shame, so we learn to avoid actions that might lead to it and long for forgiveness when we've failed.

Shame drives the "tear-and-repair" process that is vital to relationships (and that's tear as in rip, not crying). A toddler wants to stick her fingers in an electrical outlet to see what's inside. The tear happens when an adult says "no" and picks her up or steers her away, ruining the fun. The repair comes when the adult soothes the child and distracts her with something equally appealing, but safe. Repeated thousands of times, this is how the brain learns to inhibit impulses. (A smack on the hand or the bottom is not a repair; all a child learns from that is to fear the assailant.)

Schore's work focuses on shame, and he asserts that shame is the result of feeling relationally inadequate or insecurely attached. When a child is rejected by his mother, he internalizes that as shame, the feeling that "something is wrong with me." But it's a nonverbal experience, and Schore contends that it drives extreme emotional dysregulation and personality disorders.

Children who are chronically shamed by their parents are more anxious, afraid, and prone to depression. They will struggle to regulate their emotional states and may withdraw from others because they cannot tolerate the tear-and-repair process. This can also be true of children experiencing some toxically stressful situations, like the loss of a parent through divorce, incarceration, addiction, or death. In their egocentrism, these children may believe they caused the separation. The resulting core shame can have lasting impacts on relationships.

When children are misattuned with their parents, they experience the same emotional response as if they were abandoned. It's a cortisol-triggered process that stresses them just like a confrontation would. And they remember this feeling. Shame resides in the right brain, where durable, implicit memories of affective states are formed, even before the age of three. That's why children who develop core shame will be at greater risk for depression and anxiety, and will probably struggle to form other healthy relationships well into adulthood. Even learning may be difficult. Core shame can also lead to narcissism, perfectionism, a lack of empathy, and an attraction to people who confirm self-expectations.

Dr. Jay Belsky's Psychosocial Acceleration Theory ties insensitive parenting and insecure attachment to a hastened onset of puberty and sexual activity. As adults they will spend a lot of time preening and looking for short-term relationships, either exploitatively (taking what they can get, then moving on) or ambivalently (seeking love but finding it overwhelming and withdrawing).

Shame is a major theme of comedian Hannah Gadsby's groundbreaking, riveting, and at times grueling stand-up performance titled *Nanette*, which aired on Netflix. In it, she talks about growing up in Tasmania's "Bible belt" during a "toxic" national debate on legalizing homosexuality.

> Seventy percent of the people who raised me, who loved me, who I trusted, believed that homosexuality was a sin, that homosexuals were heinous, sub-human pedophiles. Seventy percent. By the time I identified as being gay, it was too late. I was already homophobic, and you do not get to just flick a switch on that. No, what you do is you internalize that homophobia and you learn to hate yourself. Hate yourself to the core. I sat soaking in shame, in the closet, for ten years. Because the closet can only stop you

from being seen. It is not shame-proof. When you soak a child in shame, they cannot develop the neurological pathways that carry thought, you know, carry thoughts of self-worth. They can't do that. Self-hatred is only ever a seed planted from outside in. But when you do that to a child, it becomes a weed so thick, and it grows so fast, the child doesn't know any different. It becomes as natural as gravity.

The Role of Reactivity

Physiological reactivity refers to bodily responses to stressful situations, and we all have a default setting for this. A child with high physiological reactivity, whether it's inherited or in response to stress, tends to move a lot, and to cry more frequently and loudly. When there is low conflict in the environment, children with high physiological reactivity will show fewer problems. Kids who are more typical, with moderate to low physiological reactivity, will seem to struggle more in a normal environment. They are going to explore. But in moments of conflict, guess who has the behavior problems? The kids who were quieter in normal situations, the ones with high physiological reactivity. So just because you see a kid behaving well in a normal environment does not mean that he or she is doing well.

All kids get into stuff. Typical kids can be redirected and can quiet themselves in moments of conflict. But children with high physiological reactivity will have more behavioral outbursts, and those outbursts will be more severe.

In a normal environment, typical kids may take the risk of getting on your nerves. They like to explore everything, including adults' tolerance limits. This is the great risk of car-seat parenting. A child with high physiological reactivity who's kept in a car seat, or otherwise restricted in movement, will not have opportunities to explore and to learn how to navigate a high-conflict environment. It's really important that we help children whose response style tends toward dysregulation learn to be a little more expressive in low-conflict environments. We need to bring them out of those low-conflict environments and let them explore, with safety and structure, so they can learn to regulate, and we can adjust their physiological reactivity.

In a classroom, the typical child will act up a little but stop when corrected by the teacher. The child with high physiological reactivity is likely to be on the periphery of the classroom activity, literally and/or figuratively; he is quiet but not engaged. But he is more likely to cause a disruption or to overreact to some other disruption.

The Curse of Perfectionism

Many years ago, I met with a mother who had brought in a four-year-old son who was hesitant to go out in public because he feared loud noises. A pediatrician had found no physical reason for the boy to be hearing-sensitive. In interviews, we determined that the mother was highly attuned to the boy's emotional state and would swoop in to soothe or correct the situation the moment she noticed that the child appeared distressed.

Children—especially bright ones, as this boy was—are prone to making erroneous cause-and-effect connections. They are superstitious. "The last time I went to that place I got scared, and so that's a scary place and I don't want to go there." In this case, the mother, in her zeal to protect her child, had inadvertently taught the boy to fear loud noises by quickly removing him from the situation every time he appeared startled or momentarily distressed, as any child will when confronted with new stimuli.

The boy understood traffic lights, so we used that as a model for building a scale of discomfort that he could communicate to his mother. Blue and green were for low stress. Yellow indicated tolerable nervousness—he would remain in the situation. In orange, he would count to three and re-evaluate, and if he still felt stressed, mom would get him away. Red was for immediate departure.

The child worked hard at this. He was not happy with leaving arenas and other places where the fun is sometimes very loud. The color-coded system gave him a way to quantify his discomfort and determine his preferred response to it. And that really was the key. The mother had nothing but the best intentions, but her interventions were preventing the experiences that would help the boy learn how to cope with tolerable stress.

We've developed this notion that any seemingly negative or even challenging experience will damage a child, but that's just not true. When a child is in an anxiety process and a parent pushes him or her toward avoidance, the child's world shrinks. And while it might be easy (if unfortunate) to avoid circuses and amusement parks and other such places, it's virtually impossible to avoid sirens, thunder, fire alarms, etc. In this case, because the mother sought help for the boy while he was still very young, we were able to help him change his physiological response to stress. Five years later, this would have been much more difficult.

In my practice I've worked with many parents who want to be perfect. As I've introduced the concept of being just good enough, they have often started to cry with relief. When mothers carry the expectation that they must never fail, then every problem feels like evidence of their insufficiency. The stress load is overwhelming. Neither marriages nor parent-child bonds can withstand the constant evaluative process of believing "I must do more, I must be perfect." This is a cortisol-driven activation process that never leads to the reward and joy of living in a loving family.

Dopamine is a neurotransmitter that drives seeking and rewards us for finding things. Cortisol, the stress hormone, can set that process in motion. Perfectionist mothers are stuck in a loop: Their high cortisol levels have them constantly chasing something that just gets farther out of reach. Without the dopaminergic reward, the cortisol level keeps rising, facilitating shame, and hindering the processes that drive nurturing and bonding. Feeling the detachment, the child may act out, giving the mother even more reason to feel like a failure and pushing her toward depression.

When we introduce the idea of being good enough, we can help mothers understand that their responsibility is to repair the fabric of the relationship, not to avoid tearing it, because that's impossible.

Perfectionism can also manifest as a fixation on the child's behavior. But the only thing children are perfect at is testing parents' limits. When parents ask me how often they should discipline, I tell them to look for opportunities to correct the behavior as often as you can, using the least amount of redirection possible. Fortunately, children provide countless opportunities for us to show them how to live happily within the limits we've imposed, and how to apply those lessons to different situations. That's what good-enough parenting is about: raising children who can grow up to love and be loved by navigating the tear-and-repair process with others.

Modulating the joy and shame processes builds the attachment commodities that we'll use for the rest of our lives. In the right circumstances, all of this occurs naturally in the child's brain. If these processes do not develop correctly, and the baby has an anxious attachment, he or she will carry that into adulthood. At that point, undoing the damage is very difficult. An adult in therapy has to work through it with the left brain in a top-down process, left hemisphere over to right hemisphere, down to limbic system and down to body. It takes about seven years of therapy to overcome an insecure attachment.

It is possible to parent using only punishment designed to prevent a recurrence of the behavior. But what does that mean? That we should break a child's arm when he reaches for something he's been told not to touch? It would "work," but it's reprehensible. Spanking and other forms of corporal punishment have been linked to increased odds, in adulthood, of depression, suicidal ideation or attempts, substance abuse, personality disorders, and abuse of others. So the goal is not to find punishments that work, but to find ways to shape and redirect.

Attunement

In presentations, I ask audience members to participate in an exercise that I learned from Bessel Van Der Kolk, a psychiatrist known for his work in posttraumatic stress. I ask everyone to split up into groups of two, with one person telling a story, any story, to the other person. When I give the signal, the listener is supposed to look down at the floor while the storyteller continues. At the next signal, a minute or so later, the listener looks up again.

At the end of the exercise, I ask the storytellers how they felt while the listener was looking down. The storytellers typically express frustration or even mild panic over feeling tuned out. Many will say that they automatically leaned forward or spoke louder to make themselves heard. Then when I ask the listeners how they felt, most will admit to feeling some level of guilt or regret for adopting a posture of not listening.

The storytellers in that exercise perform a predominately left-brain function, recounting a memory in a linear narrative. The listeners are using their right brains, conjuring mental images based on their interpretations of the storyteller's words. When the connection between the two is broken, both people struggle. The executive functions of the storyteller's prefrontal left brain get distracted by limbic processes of the right brain, which is suddenly anxious over the listener's lack of nonverbal cues. The storyteller suddenly feels insecure.

Listeners experience something similar. Upon looking down, they are aware of doing something they shouldn't be doing. Their bodies produce a negative, self-critical, affective state—even when they are following directions in a game!

Imagine, then, the stress of a disconnected relationship. Children who grow up in toxic stress vacillate between those two states. They are constantly distracted by their emotional experiences stemming from not feeling connected and attached. Later in life, when they seek out relationships, the may struggle to connect, and that overwhelms them with shame all over again.

We are hardwired to connect using our faces and reflecting that process through our bodies. There's a reason that smiles for photographs often don't look convincing. When you experience joy or laughter, it doesn't just raise the muscles around your mouth; it crinkles the muscles around your eyes. The third, fifth, and seventh cranial nerves constrict the muscles around your eyes, and this also lifts the muscles around the edges of your mouth, pulling it into that familiar upward curve. When the muscles around the eyes are not constricted, the upturned mouth looks odd. Try it in a mirror.

In mammals, baring teeth is usually a sign of aggression. In humans, showing the teeth in a smile is incidental to what's really going on. It's our eyes that communicate. When the muscles around the eyes crinkle, the whites of our eyes become less visible—the opposite of the widening that occurs when we're startled or frightened. Dogs, which have evolved to live with us, are very good at reading our eyes. In fact, they're better at it than chimpanzees. This is why dogs don't look where we point—they're focused on our eyes, trying to discern our mood and meaning.

Not coincidentally, the same cranial nerves that cause eye-crinkling all end in the nucleus accumbens, which sits behind the prefrontal cortex and serves as a connection point to two other important processes: a dopaminergic process (dopamine is a neurotransmitter) that is fed from the ventral tegmental area, which is involved in addiction and love; and the tenth cranial nerve. Also called the vagus nerve, it activates everything from your gastrointestinal tract to your trachea and chin area. It's like emotional radar for your brain. There are four to six times as many neuronal processes running from the body to the brain as there are running from the brain to the body. The body tells you what you are feeling, including emotions. This is why our feelings are often evident in our faces. Even when we try to mask this, people who know us well can tell. This is how we communicate: Body to face, and face to body. That builds the capacity to recognize cues for safety and danger, and to co-regulate or emotions with others'.

These processes build an interpersonal neurobiology narrative that says "these people are safe and I am loved." Think about the benefits you get from your loving relationships. Someone who loves you will tell you that you did something wrong but not threaten to leave you. That's a resilient relationship. It can handle tear and repair, distance and closeness, and can navigate intimacy. People in a relationship like that can state their needs and wants and accept the occasional "no." They understand that they will make mistakes, small regrets, but also a commitment—possibly unspoken—that there will be no big regrets. "There are things I will never do. I don't have to spell those out, but you can trust me never to hurt you so severely that we can't heal the wound." That's a resilient relationship.

You want to take a similar structure with all your important relationships. Even a healthy and productive employee-employer relationship requires trust and the understanding that certain violations will force a severing of the relationship.

Whether from fiction or real life, we're all familiar with the mother who expressed undying love for a child as he's led away to prison. And that mother does love her child. But it's different now. Because he did something that he and his mother had agreed, either explicitly or tacitly, that he would never do. All relationships have a breaking point. You may still care about the person who has violated your trust, but it is no longer a resilient relationship.

We have to build resilient relationships that can tolerate tear and repair, that can deal with conflict and resolution, that can share joy, that communicate care, that aren't derailed by rage or panic or fear. And we have to equip others to build the same relationships, and that's why coaching is such an important part of helping adults become mentors.

If adults are going to help youth, they have to learn how to coach. Coaching is different from parenting or teaching. In general, parents are quick to yell and teachers are quick to tell. But neither yelling nor telling builds relationships—that is in the doing. And so as we talk about building resiliency, we have to be mindful of what resilient relationships look like. Ultimately, a resilient relationship can deal with significant levels of stress without breaking and, in fact, can offset the stress through support. No relationship can help us avoid stress, but resilient relationships can help us navigate it.

Incidentally, contrary to popular opinion, self-esteem does not have significant impact on mental-health status or life performance. What matters is self-efficacy. Knowing your abilities and limitations is far more helpful than believing you're good at everything.

Richard Weissbourd, a child and family psychologist at Harvard's Graduate School of Education, asserts that children need certain positive experiences to ground themselves in a healthy, moral state. One of the claims that Weissbourd makes is that it's more important for a child to be known than to be praised. Children know when they've done well and when they haven't, and they recognize phony praise. Praise resonates when the child feels that the person demonstrates awareness of her skills and struggles.

We need to help children understand that everyone has talents and challenges so that they can deal insightfully with their own flaws. Honesty helps them mature. Children who don't receive honest, constructive feedback fail to become reflective and will be prone to either unwarranted pride or crushing shame. When we demonstrate a capacity to change our behavior after feedback and/or self-reflection, we model vital aspects of maturity: dealing with difficult feelings such as frustration and disappointment; controlling anger toward others; and seeing ourselves from others' perspectives.

"Nurture" Matters More Than "Nature"

You may have learned in school that genes are like blueprints, but that's not quite right. They're more like rough schematics accompanied by extensive notes on variables, depending on the conditions in which the "construction" takes place. Those conditions are determined by our environments, especially in the first few years of life. This is why preventing interference with brain development in the early years is vital not just for the individual, but for the children that individual might have someday. The damage lives in our very cells.

We are not exactly like our parents. We inherit 50 percent of our genetic load from each parent, but only half of your genetic load is expressed (switched on) in your genotype, the precise combination of expressed genes that makes you, you. We're all around 25 percent of each of our parents, in terms of gene expression. You are born with certain propensities or temperaments that generate personality. There is debate over how flexible personality is, but we know that personality is not well manifested until age two and a half. What informs that process is which half of your inherited DNA is going to stand up, and which half will go to sleep. What is expressed is determined by experience.

In a chapter left out of his book *The Sports Gene*, but later excerpted online, David Epstein describes the nascent field of epigenetics, the study of gene expression. The word epigenetics means "above genes" and refers to the fact that information not encoded in DNA is somehow passed down. This happens through a couple of processes, including methylation, in which new molecules are added to the DNA strand, affecting what it does and when.

Through epigenetics, we've learned that experiences can be passed down, in a manner of speaking. To illustrate the point, Epstein writes about the Nazi occupation of the Netherlands in 1944–45, and the famine that resulted in the northwestern part of the country, which came to be known as the Dutch Hunger Winter. But the end of the war was not the end of the story. Epstein explains:

> Six decades later, an international group of scientists tracked down the children of women who were pregnant during that famine—as well as the children of Dutch women who were in provinces not struck by famine—and looked at a gene known as the insulin-like growth factor 2, or IGF2. The gene plays a key role in body growth and development. The subjects whose mothers were in the early stages of pregnancy during the Dutch Hunger Winter had fewer 'turn off' signaling methyl molecules attached to their IGF2 genes compared to their siblings . . . . So, some six decades after a brief period of intense famine, adults whose

mothers were exposed at just the wrong time of pregnancy carried the mark of the Dutch Hunger Winter attached to their DNA.

Other studies have found similar results. But the effects apparently are not limited to physical traits.

Epstein continues:

> Some of the more mind-boggling results are coming from behavior studies. In 1999, a team of neuroscientists conducted an experiment in rats in which they took the offspring of mother rats that had been bred to be nervous and not very nurturing—less licking and grooming—and put them with mother mice that had been bred to be calm and nurturing. The adopted rats grew up more calm and adventurous and nurtured their own offspring akin to how their adoptive mothers had raised them. The team found that the nurturing in the first few weeks of life permanently turned certain genes up and down in the brain that made the adoptees more resilient to stress. And the mental tranquility was passed down to the adoptees' offspring as well.
>
> In the closest thing to a human equivalent, researchers at the Traumatic Stress Studies Division of the Mount Sinai Medical Centre in New York City tracked women who were pregnant on 9/11 and in the vicinity of the attacks. Some of the women later developed post-traumatic stress disorder, particularly those who had lower levels of the hormone cortisol, which is protective in stressful situations. Specifically, the women who were in the third trimester of pregnancy on 9/11 had babies with low cortisol levels. This area of science

> needs far more work to provide solid conclusions, but the researchers think that epigenetic marks, set in place by the events of a single day at just the right (or wrong) moment during pregnancy, may be responsible.

Newborns are not exempt from the effect. Research at the University of British Columbia and BC Children's Hospital Research Institute found that "children who had been more distressed as infants and had received less physical contact had a molecular profile in their cells that was underdeveloped for their age, pointing to the possibility that they were lagging biologically. Scientists found consistent methylation differences between high-contact and low-contact children at five specific DNA sites. Two of these sites fall within genes: one plays a role in the immune system, and the other is involved in metabolism."

Epstein warns, "To say that the study of epigenetics is in its infancy would be to exaggerate how far along it is." But we do know most of our DNA plays no role in who we are. Only about 20 percent is related to your height, hair, or eye color, shape of your nose, etc.; the other 80 percent of your DNA tells the 20 percent how to express itself—the notes accompanying the schematic—through DNA methylation.

Telomeres are chemical structures attached to strands of DNA molecules. They function like the zipper on your jacket, locking the strands together so that chromosomes match up properly. Every time a cell replicates, the telomeres are affected. Over time, they get shorter and shorter, until they are so short that they cannot match. At that point, the cell cannot replicate. (This is one of the key aging processes in our bodies.) Toxic stress attacks telomeres. People who experience significant levels of toxic stress have an increased propensity for telomeric breakdown, and therefore fewer generations of cell reproduction. This is how toxic stress can so affect biology that it changes the way the person's DNA works.

Twin studies show us that genes are not destiny. Identical twins can differ in noticeable ways, like height or age at which baldness sets in. They're born with the same DNA, but their experiences, in utero and post-utero, change the manifestation of that DNA as it presents in that person. When one identical twin has schizophrenia, the odds of the other twin having it are about 50 percent. That's far higher than the risk in the general population, but much less than the 100 percent we'd expect if genes alone determined everything about our health.

Stress can have enormous influence on the processes that determine which genes are switched on and which remain silent, and that influence can touch future generations. These changes can be reversed, but only if experience turns off the DNA process.

CHAPTER 4

Prison Without Bars: The Stress of Isolation

"Nine times out of 10, the story behind the misbehavior won't make you angry; it will break your heart."

—Annette Breaux

In an essay in the *New York Times* titled "No One Helped My Mentally Ill Mother, or Me," writer Laura Zera recounted growing up simultaneously hoping and fearing that her family's dark secret would be discovered.

"My mother was a master of artifice, and her illness went undetected, too. She spent an inordinate amount of energy to appear typical. She held down a job, cooked healthy meals, drove me to figure skating practices and volunteered at my school. Her rage erupted at times in front of my friends' parents, and my teachers and coaches, especially when she stood rinkside and screamed about my improperly positioned arms and legs. But if her conduct set off alarm bells, nobody said anything.

"What could they have said? The odds of initiating a constructive conversation with a shell-shocked adolescent or her defensive mother were minuscule. But the child in me still collapses from the imprinted sorrow of years of isolation. It pains me that people thought we were OK, and we weren't. Or, they didn't think we were OK, and opted not to speak up. What good are manners when someone is suffering?"

Family isolation is one of the great ironies of our transition away from hunter-gatherer communities. Our numbers have exploded across the globe, but we've never been more alone. We are separated not just by walls and yards, but by largely unspoken mores against meddling in other people's personal business.

In his 2002 report on the effects of neglect, Dr. Bruce Perry of the ChildTrauma Academy in Houston, Texas, includes a chart showing the change in the size of the typical "household" in Western societies from 10,000 BC to AD 2000. The decrease is sharp, from clans of around 40 in our prehistoric, hunter-gatherer days, to less than three in the typical American home 12,000 years later. Perry writes:

> Our brain evolved over hundreds of thousands of generations in hominid and prehominid social groups. A dependent child grew up in the presence of the elderly, siblings, adults—related and not. There was a more continuous exposure and wider variety of socio-emotional interactions. The child in this situation had many opportunities to form relationships and, in a use-dependent way, develop the capacity to have a rich array of relationships.
>
> We are now raising children in environments that are very different from the rich social context for which our

> brains are most suited. The effects of television and other electronic activities have significantly exacerbated this. Taking huge portions of the available day away from socio-emotional or other 'human' activities, television ensures that new—and non-social—neural systems are being activated in comparison with humans raised one hundred years ago. The implications of this have yet to be fully understood.

Speaking to NPR on the same topic, Alison Gopnik, a psychology and philosophy professor at the University of California, Berkeley, said, "For as long as we've been human, the whole village has been involved in caring for children. By the time you were ready to have children yourself, you'd had lots of practical experience in caring for children."

In the 20th century, as families got smaller and more insular, "For the first time, people were having children who hadn't had much experience of caring for children but had lots of experience of going to school and working. It was kind of natural for people to think, 'OK, this is like going to school and working. And if I can just find the right manual or the right secret handbook, I'm going to succeed at this task the same way that I succeeded in my classes or I succeeded at my job."

That's how "parent" became a verb, and "parenting" a job from which only the most egregiously unqualified are ever fired. And as in our work settings, we are quicker to judge colleagues' performances than to offer to help when they're overwhelmed. It seems similar to the disgust response discussed in Chapter 1. But instead of disease, we're afraid of contracting other people's psychological challenges or financial misfortunes. Whatever the case, isolation cuts us off from processes that are important to development.

Learning to Dance

Parents of more than one child, I'm going to reveal your secret: You love your children equally, but you do not like them equally. There is no shame in this; it's just the way we are. You have different resonances, different relational tendencies with your children—and it's supposed to be that way. Temperamental matches and mismatches are important for development. The word I often use for this is *dance.*

When you see the child that's most like you doing things that you used to do, it aggravates you. You believe you know—and you're probably right—what wheels are turning in the child's head, possibly even more clearly than the child does. Seeing and dealing with those attributes that remind us of ourselves, at least as we were at that age, is aggravating.

And you will naturally feel differently about a child who is more like your significant other, a person whom you love, whose personality is comforting to you, and whose mistakes and flaws you forgive. You've worked out what couples' therapists call complementarity with your partner, and you extend that feeling to a child who reminds you of that partner.

Children are not exact duplicates of us, of course. They will tend to show traits from both parents, but more often than not, they'll more closely align with the temperament of one parent. And some of a child's traits may be inherited from a grandparent, further complicating our interactions.

My father was a Pentecostal preacher and a mechanical engineer, and as a teenager, I drove him crazy. I scored well on academic assessment tests but consistently earned Ds in my classes. I wasn't oppositional—I just didn't care. School didn't interest me. I preferred to joke around and talk to girls. And because we were Pentecostal, I figured grades didn't matter because Jesus was coming. But that was a rationalization for my inability or unwillingness to focus on tasks. Dad would tell me to clean the garage. When he checked in hours later, he would find that the only change was that the newspapers were neatly stacked because I'd read the comics all day. He would get frustrated, yell, and tell me again to clean the garage the next day, with similar results.

Interestingly, I learned later, my dad couldn't clean the garage either. He would rearrange his tools all day. He'd also flunked out quickly during his first attempt at college. But then he served in World War II and came out a different person, serious and focused. He earned a degree at Ohio State and married my mother, whom he'd been in love with since second grade.

Then I came along, the third child and the first to remind him of his own youthful frivolity. He didn't want me to have to go to war, as he had, to get my head straight. It's entirely possible he would have changed anyway as he got older and his prefrontal cortex matured. But he didn't know that and so he carried relational anxiety about me. He loved me, but he couldn't figure out how to get me from where I was to where he wanted me to be. What got me there was other relationships.

My brother was more like our mother, and he and my father got along well. My brother could clean the garage, and he taught me. I also had my mother, my grandparents, and my sisters, and I danced differently with each of them. I had a constellation of relationships to navigate, experiencing tears and repairs, and learning as I grew. If I clashed with any of them, I had another person with whom to discuss it. They all mentored me in relationships.

Then, like my father, I matured a lot in my early twenties, and he and I were very close until he died. But it took getting through that adjustment period by being able to dance with another temperamental style, another relational process that was not the same as mine. By navigating tear-and-repair processes with my brother, I was able to able forge a stronger relationship with my father. And my garage is clean and organized.

Temperamental match isn't only about conflict, like some grand prank nature plays on parents. The flip side of the aggravation is attunement, the intuitive, nonverbal awareness of what's going on in the other person's head; and empathy, the capacity to act on or express that understanding. That attunement drives our attachment to and protectiveness of our children.

And grandchildren. As we discussed earlier, we inherit 25 percent of our genes from each parent; the other 50 percent comes from our grandparents. As we discussed earlier, this is why humans have evolved to live well past our viable reproductive years—because having another set of adults around with a vested interested in a child's survival and maturity gave us an evolutionary advantage. The temperamental dance is part of that process. And that's why grandparents raising grandchildren is not ideal. When a grandparent has to step into a parental role, the child loses an important relationship mentor, someone who knows both the child and the child's parent and can teach dance moves that no one else can.

But the dance is not just for familial relationships—those

are practice for the larger world. Children who don't start to develop these skills within a family will struggle with relationships throughout life.

So Close and Yet So Far

Hillary Clinton's book *It Takes a Village to Raise a Child* was controversial when it was published in 1996. Some saw the philosophy expressed in the title as challenging the primacy of the family. At the Republican National Convention that year, presidential nominee Senator Bob Dole said, "It doesn't take a village to raise a child; it takes a family to raise a child."

Or, as then-First Lady Barbara Bush had put it in her address to Wellesley College grads in 1990, "You must read to your children, hug your children, and you must love your children. Your success as a family . . . our success as a society depends not on what happens in the White House, but on what happens inside your house."

That's absolutely correct. Unfortunately, not all children are as blessed as I was, or as you may feel if you grew up with two loving parents, extended family, friends and neighbors and others you could go to for help, even if you never had to. Families living in poverty, or beset with an abusive parent, addiction, or mental illness, are more likely to be socially isolated. Isolation is fundamentally damaging to all group mammals. It drives depression and disassociation. Babies left alone too long will just stop crying, out of despair as well as exhaustion. Children growing up in isolated homes will have few dance partners, perhaps only one, and that adult may have his or her own relational challenges.

Children raised in insulated, isolated, single-parent homes tend to have significantly more behavioral problems and lower academic achievement. They are three times more likely to demonstrate negative psychological well-being through emotional-behavioral disturbances. But it's important to understand that socioeconomic status plays an important role in this.

In isolated homes, parents often will become more focused on behavior—whether the child is obeying or disobeying—than on nurturing. These parents may set expectations so high that they and their children live with the constant anxiety of perceived failures over clashes or disappointments that they don't realize are inevitable. They work so hard not to tear the relationship that they don't learn the limits of it.

The point of relational processes is tear and repair. If you're always tearing because the child is just like you, or if you're too quick to repair because the child is not like you, or if the single mother is always torn because the child reminds her so much of her estranged husband, the dance rhythm never varies and the child is stuck. By having a second temperamental style in the home, the child gets to navigate the tear-and-repair process. The child can steer clear of you when you're angry but still experience closeness with the other adult.

Fathers

Moms send their children two basic messages: Please don't do that, but I will love you anyway. The message from fathers, in the first decade, is: I'm a little scary, but we'll have fun together. Later, the message becomes: I am dangerous, follow my rules or you're out of here.

Fathers tend to play with their children a little more roughly than mothers do—chasing, wrestling, "airplane rides," etc. Some mothers are disturbed by this, but injuries are rare. Rough-and-tumble play is important for development—it helps children practice their motor skills, bond with their caregivers (which we'll discuss later in the book) and, perhaps most important, begin to understand the limits and consequences of behavior. And because other children like physical play, those who are exposed to it at home are often more popular among their peers. This is how we start to develop not just interpersonal skills but learn how to take turns, what's fair and not fair, agreeing to and abiding by rules, etc. Ethical development is grounded in the play that dominates the first ten years or so of our lives, and fathers play a key role in that.

Children growing up without a father are at greater risk for antisocial behavior. Boys who grow up without fathers often exhibit increased promiscuity and criminality as well as a general increase in macho behaviors.

Girls growing up without a father have increased rates of teenage sexual activity and pregnancy. This was true in hunter-gatherer communities as well. In hunter-gatherer communities in which fathers are present and involved, girls begin menstruation later, will begin having sex later, and will have fewer sex partners, compared to communities in which fathers are not involved. Presumably this is because the involved father restricts his daughter's movements, interfering with the environmental factors—like being around a lot of unrelated males—that trigger hormones.

And the effects seem to get worse over time. In his book *Safe House: How Emotional Safety Is the Key to Raising Kids Who Live, Love, and Lead Well*, Dr. Joshua Straub reports: "A team of researchers at the Johns Hopkins School of Medicine set out on a thirty-year study to find if a single related cause existed for five major issues: mental illness, hypertension, malignant tumors, coronary heart disease, and suicide. After studying 1,377 students over thirty years, the most prevalent single cause wasn't what everyone thought. They found that the most significant predictor of these tragedies was a lack of closeness to the parents, especially the father."

When parents are together but not securely attached, they are in general more promiscuous, less committed, and less responsive to and supportive of their children. This can lead to children exaggerating their need for care and attention—acting out—in order to get a response.

The research on stepfathers is less conclusive. Some findings suggest that a series of father-like figures is problematic for development. Broadly speaking, children living with a stepfather are forty times more likely to be abused as those living with two genetic parents, but this statistic can be misleading. When you control for socioeconomic status, that gap shrinks dramatically.

Research strongly indicates that children are better off with two adults in the home. The research does not suggest that those adults must be one male and one female, or of the same generation, or married or related to each other. It's more about the relational dance and providing the children with different temperaments and styles to navigate. Two parents tend to take on shared responsibilities. As long as one is more nurturing and one is more protective, it doesn't matter if they are male and female. The protective parent does not necessarily need to be a male.

That's why a single mother with three children is better off raising them with another single mother with her own three children, so that two adults are handling these six children. Two dance partners are just better than one.

Three, four, ten, better still. In an interview with The Knowledge Project podcast, economist and author Tyler Cowen advised parents to expose their teenagers "to as many of your friends who might be role models as possible," in order to help them find their place in the world. "Your influence [as a parent] is limited, for better or worse."

This is why we must help families build networks of support. We must equip families to get together, be together, build social networks, and allow a community network to develop in areas where toxic stress is most impactful. That process of mutual support starts to drive change.

Poverty

For her 1998 book *Nickel and Dimed: On (Not) Getting By in America*, journalist Barbara Ehrenreich went undercover, so to speak, in working-class America. She took low-skill jobs in several states, then wrote about her experiences, including the endless calculations involved in trying to cover rent, food, and transportation costs, plus unexpected expenses, on minimum wage. In the final chapter, she notes the disconnect between what most Americans believe about work, and what millions of their fellow citizens endure every day:

> According to a recent poll conducted by Jobs for the Future, a Boston-based employment research firm, 94 percent of Americans agree that 'people who work full-time

> should be able to earn enough to keep their families out of poverty.' I grew up hearing over and over, to the point of tedium, that 'hard work' was the secret of success: 'Work hard and you'll get ahead' or 'It's hard work that got us where we are.' No one ever said that you could work hard—harder even than you ever thought possible—and still find yourself sinking ever deeper into poverty and debt.

Poverty grinds people down, and children are not immune. Indeed, for many, perhaps most children, to grow up poor is to be sentenced to a lifetime of struggle. In 2017, *Mother Jones* magazine wrote about work by neuroscientists Kimberly Noble and Martha Farah and others to build a "neurocognitive profile" of socioeconomic status and the developing brain.

> In one study Farah looked at 283 MRIs and found that kids from poorer, less-educated families tended to have thinner sub-regions of the prefrontal cortex—a part of the brain strongly associated with executive functioning—than better-off kids. . . . In 2015, Noble co-authored the largest study to date. Using MRI, researchers examined 1,099 children and young adults and found that the brains of those with higher family income and more parental education had larger surface areas than their poorer, less-educated peers. Children from families making less than $25,000 suffered the most, with 6 percent less brain surface area than peers in families making $150,000 or more.
>
> A few months later, another large study co-authored by Seth Pollak, a child psychologist at the University of Wisconsin-Madison, found strong ties between household income and the volume of gray matter in the fron-

> tal lobe, temporal lobe, and hippocampus. Children from households below the federal poverty line ($24,250 for a family of four in 2015) had 8 to 10 percent less gray matter in these critical regions. And even kids whose families were slightly better off—incomes of one and a half times the federal poverty level—had 3 to 4 percent less gray matter than the developmental norm. In Pollak's study, many of the poor parents were highly educated, indicating that the 'maturational lags' their children suffered from were a direct result of the circumstances of poverty.

It's important to note, however, that poverty does not drive stress. Inequality drives stress. This is an important distinction. In areas in the world in which everyone is poor, you don't necessarily find elevated levels of cortisol in people. But toxic stress thrives in places where there is pronounced and noticeable income inequality, where there is poverty amid plenty. That is where poverty is a strong predictor of toxic stress, poor health, and the kind of social isolation that can exacerbate both.

Poverty dramatically diminishes one's resilience to stress and capacity to be open to relationships that would offset stress, and in this way it becomes self-perpetuating. The experience of poverty narrows the "bandwidth" for one's application of self-regulation, one of the core processes that drive our ability to achieve goals and take care of others. When your skills are focused on survival, you lose the capacity to focus on the future. As Sendhil Mullainathan and Eldar Shafir explain in their book *Scarcity: Why Having Too Little Means So Much*:

> Juggling public transportation, childcare, changing job shifts, caring for family on a limited budget, and navigating

> public assistance requirements, for instance, requires a high degree of organization, multi-tasking, inhibition, and emotional control. Using so many self-regulation resources to attend to the daily tasks of living leaves fewer resources for other purposes. In addition, poverty may also lead to 'tunneling,' or the tendency of people to focus intensively on their most pressing sources of financial stress and short-term needs at the expense of future needs. Tunneling can lead a person to make short-term decisions that alleviate urgent needs but cause greater financial challenges in the long run.

If you're having a fight with your significant other, is that the time to plan your wedding or a vacation? Of course not. The stress of the argument keeps you focused on the moment (and possibly the past as you dredge up other times he or she has angered you). And if a simple argument with someone you love can dominate your attention to the exclusion of all else, think about how much more the ongoing struggle for literal survival can interfere with every aspect of one's life.

Racism

In 2017, Dr. Roberto Montenegro, Chief Fellow at Seattle Children's Hospital at the University of Washington, told NPR about an incident that prompted him to study race and stress. After earning his Ph.D. at UCLA, colleagues took Montenegro and his wife out to celebrate. When he left the restaurant, he was mistaken for a valet by white people. Twice. "I vividly remember turning red," he recalled. "And I remember my heart pounding." These, of course, are stress responses.

Montenegro went on to earn an M.D. as well, and today he is part of a small but growing movement to understand the physical effects of racism. "Individually these incidents seem benign," he said. "But cumulatively I believe that they act like sort of low-grade micro-traumas that can that end up hurting you and your biology. It's not just having your feelings hurt. It's having your biology hurt as well."

In 2006, Laura Smart Richman, an associate professor at Duke University, was studying the relationship between identity and stress when an unexpected development added a new dimension to her research: An African-American woman accused members of the Duke lacrosse team of rape, and the national media descended. After this story, Richman saw higher cortisol levels in her black experiment volunteers, especially women. "The findings suggest that recent exposure to race-related stress can have a sustained impact on physiological stress responses," she wrote.

For many years we've assumed that socioeconomic factors accounted for the disparities between whites and people of color in heart disease, obesity, infant mortality, life expectancy, and an array of other conditions. But new research is showing that income and opportunity imbalances cannot explain it away.

The news site ProPublica reported in 2017 that

> A black woman is 22 percent more likely to die from heart disease than a white woman, 71 percent more likely to perish from cervical cancer, but 243 percent more likely to die from pregnancy- or childbirth-related causes. What's more, even relatively well-off black women . . . die or nearly die at higher rates than whites. . . . A 2016 analysis of five

years of data [from New York City] found that black college-educated mothers who gave birth in local hospitals were more likely to suffer severe complications of pregnancy or childbirth than white women who never graduated from high school.

In the more than 200 stories of African-American mothers that ProPublica and NPR have collected over the past year, the feeling of being devalued and disrespected by medical providers was a constant theme. . . . Arline Geronimus, a professor at the University of Michigan School of Public Health, coined the term 'weathering' for how this continuous stress wears away at the body. Weathering 'causes a lot of different health vulnerabilities and increases susceptibility to infection,' she said, 'but also early onset of chronic diseases, in particular, hypertension and diabetes'—conditions that disproportionately affect blacks at much younger ages than whites. It accelerates aging at the cellular level; in a 2010 study, Geronimus and colleagues found that the telomeres (chromosomal markers of aging) of black women in their 40s and 50s appeared 7 1/2 years older on average than those of whites."

Many blamed weathering for the January 2018 death of police-reform activist Erica Garner following a heart attack at age twenty-seven. Garner's father Eric had died in a struggle with police in 2014, and his story was the source of the "I can't breathe!" slogan used at many Black Lives Matter rallies.

"When has racism not killed?" kihana miraya ross, a postdoctoral fellow at the University of Texas at Austin Institute for Urban Policy Research & Analysis, wondered in an interview with Vice.com. "Whether that's in the form of outright murder as in the case of Erica Garner's father, or health related or even black-on-black crime that stems from racialized capitalism, racialized housing disparities, and the numerous traumas both individual and collective that come from existing as the antithesis to everything pure, clean, and white—being raced as black has always killed us."

Artificial Joy

There is a cruel irony in addiction. The same hardwiring that compels us to seek love, care, and joy with others, over and over, is vulnerable to hijacking by alcohol, drugs, and even some behaviors. All addictive substances, with the possible exception of marijuana, impact our naturally occurring opioids on some level. That's why all humans are potentially susceptible to addiction. The addict's love for the substance or behavior replaces the desire to love or be loved.

Through most of human history, the addictive substances available to us were not nearly as powerful as the heroin and medicinal opioids available today, hence the addiction crisis that is devastating communities—especially poor ones—across the country. But we are all surrounded by addicting substances and activities. Gambling and video games can release the same levels of endogenous opioids as addictive substances, activating the nucleus accumbens into a seeking process. Even checking your cell phone triggers an endogenous opioid reward, and when you misplace your phone you experience a cortisol response.

Limiting or eliminating exposure to "artificial" joy experiences—especially drugs, alcohol, and obsessive sexual behaviors—can enhance the greater group and reinforce the natural joy that comes from relationships. Excessive exposure undermines personal relational capacities and impedes the natural human need for nurturing relationships.

In a 2013 study, Laura Lander, an addiction therapist and assistant professor at West Virginia University, writes, "Each family and each family member is uniquely affected by the individual using substances, including but not limited to having unmet developmental needs, impaired attachment, economic hardship, legal problems, emotional distress, and sometimes violence being perpetrated against him or her."

Ironically, excessive use of social media can leave people feeling less connected to the larger world. *In Emotions, Learning, and the Brain: Exploring the Educational Implications of Affective Neuroscience*, Mary Helen Immordino-Yang writes:

> One recent study of more than 2,300 young adults (Canadian college students 18–22 years of age) . . . found that higher levels of social texting among research participants were weakly but consistently positively associated with out-group prejudice and materialism, for example, with reporting lower positivity toward indigenous Canadians and with believing that physical attractiveness is an important personal value.
>
> The somewhat alarming implication, still not directly tested, is that if youths are habitually pulled into the outside world by distracting media snippets, or if their primary mode of socially interacting is via brief, digitally transmitted communications, they may be systematically undermining opportunities to reflect on the moral and longer-term implication of social situations and personal

values. This situation could potentially alter the perceived quality of their social relationships and over time might bias identity development toward focusing on concrete or physical abilities, traits, and accomplishments.

CHAPTER 5

Where Do We Go from Here?

"Love is at the root of everything. All learning. All relationships. Love or the lack of it."

—Fred Rogers

Have you ever wondered why we can't tickle ourselves? Or why we're ticklish at all?

"Tickle is the primal stimulus for laughter," explained Robert Provine, a neuroscientist at the University of Maryland, in a 2017 interview with the BBC. "In fact, 'feign tickle' is my candidate for the world's most ancient joke. The 'I'm gonna get you,' threatening-to-tickle behavior. It's the only joke you can tell to both human babies and chimpanzees."

So why do we laugh?

To answer this question (which Plato once wrestled with), Provine collected more than a thousand recordings of naturally occurring laughter. In a 2000 report titled *Laughter: A Scientific Investigation* (which he later expanded into a book by the same name), he revealed the most surprising finding from this field work: Very little laughter is in response to something intentionally humorous. "Most of the laughter seemed to follow rather banal remarks, such as 'Look, it's Andre,' 'Are you sure?' and 'It was nice meeting you too.' Even our 'greatest hits,' the funniest of the 1,200 pre-laugh comments, were not necessarily howlers. . . . Mutual playfulness, in-group feeling and positive emotional tone—not comedy—mark the social settings of most naturally occurring laughter."

Laughter is social. It's a neat little trick nature came up with to bring us closer together. Yes, it can be weaponized and used to humiliate and exclude, but we all recognize that derisive laughter is cruel, even if we participate in it from time to time. On the whole it's a force for good. I think most people would agree that children's laughter is one of the most wonderful sounds in the world.

Fortunately, laughter is not the only tool we have at our disposal to help us navigate this complex, challenging, and often dangerous world we've created. We may still be learning how to adapt, after evolving in a radically different environment, but we can do better than we have, starting now.

Using Joy to Strengthen Bonds

Children have a natural propensity to build their relationships with adults. But to enhance the discipline processes in a family, we have to build the joy processes first.

Pure joy comes from relationships that provide trust, understanding, fun, and care. When there is not enough love, joy, and hope in one's life, there is no purpose to seek the good stuff that comes with being cared for and loved. Jaak Panksepp calls this good stuff "anticipation eagerness," which brings about feelings of excitement and gives humans (and other mammals) something to look forward to, something to seek. When children experience toxic stress, the "want to" and "I can" urges that drive humans to seek positive feelings are underactive, inducing a sense of hopelessness.

According to Panksepp, play is the ancestral source of authentic social joy and laughter in all mammals. From a young age, children and other mammals engage in rough and tumble play, leading to empathetic behaviors such as laughter. This social form of play often presents itself as play-fighting but is in actuality joyous. When my dogs wrestle playfully, they will take turns rolling onto their backs in the vulnerable "underdog" position. Giving and receiving trust contributes to the joy of playing.

Children should play every day! Panksepp describes play as an essential ingredient in the "daily social diet" of all children through grade school, as it is imperative to developing a healthy social brain. Play should be unstructured, involve rough and tumble aspects, and should be initiated at home by caregivers. At a young age, infant-caregiver play is crucial, as a child's early life is mostly made up of pure social interactions, predominantly with their caregivers. It is in these intense playful interactions that children begin to learn sounds, experience physical movements, learn to read, and produce facial expressions, eye gestures, and gazing.

Play allows children to explore what is and is not permitted within their communities. It prompts them to initiate, maintain, terminate, and avoid interactions with others, setting them up to build healthy connections throughout their lives. It drives children to navigate social possibilities in an enjoyable manner, allowing them to learn the impact of their behavior and their behavioral limits, develop empathy, and become high-functioning social beings.

It's important to note that competition plays no role in the kind of play we're talking about. Children do like to compete, and games with winners and losers can be fun, but that type of play has less of a role in the foundational development of emotional and social skills. Organized sports also offer important benefits, but again, they are not a replacement for play. And even in that realm, some are concerned that an emphasis on coach-guided practice over unstructured play is hampering athletic development. John O'Sullivan, founder of Changing the Game Project, a nonprofit dedicated to "return[ing] youth sports to our children," writes on his blog, "At the very core of great athletes is a burning passion and love of the game. . . . Play instills this type of love and makes it fun, while practice often does not. Instilling love of the game early on sets up a player mentally to engage in deliberate practice later on."

Interoception, Sympathy, and Empathy

Interoception is our capacity to consciously receive information from our bodies. In relationships, there is a lot of stuff that happens outside our awareness, and before we can be attuned and empathic, we must experience interoceptive awareness. When we're aware of what's going on in our bodies, we're better able to sense what's going on in someone else's body.

Interoception is what allows us to feel sympathy. We are hardwired for this skill, which chimps and bonobos share. In his book *The Bonobo and The Atheist: In Search of Humanism Among the Primates*, Frans de Waal tells a story about a bonobo that found a wounded bird and tried to gently toss it into the air to help it fly. When this failed, she took the bird up into a tree and held its wings open, as if to encourage it. When the bird fluttered to the ground, she climbed back down and sat with it, keeping the other bonobos away, until later that evening, when the bird was able to fly on its own.

Sympathy is a right-brain process. We don't need words to feel it. Think about the last time you spoke to a friend or relative who had just lost someone very close. In those situations, words seem inadequate. We hug because it's a body-to-body connection.

Empathy does not come to us as easily, and it manifests in different ways. We already have in our brains a mirror neuronal process that builds social and emotional awareness around behavioral chains. If you were to see me hold up a bottle of Diet Coke, you would build a behavioral chain around it—meaning you would have a sense of what I can do with the bottle. And if I remove the lid, take a drink and exhale contentedly, you will have an empathic experience even before I start moving. You knew what I was going to do. You were attuned to my actions. Many other mammals do this, too. Brain-imaging tests have shown that when a gorilla sees another gorilla drinking water, the first gorilla's mirror neuronal processes light up as if it too were drinking water.

If you were to see me take someone else's Diet Coke bottle and drink from it, you might have an empathic experience with that person. You might also feel revulsion. We're hardwired for shared "ick" responses when social rules are violated.

In fact we are hardwired for many relational capacities; we just have to awaken them. We have to turn down our vulnerabilities to feeling unsafe and unsupported. We have to build social connectedness because, when we do so, our bodies and brains are built to love each other. It is that loving process that will change our communities, but we have to get in touch with it, or we will remain in chronic toxic stress experiences.

We establish who is us and who is them based on two scales: warmth and competence. Warmth is our perception of whether other people are allies or enemies, and competence refers to our assessment of how effective they might be at helping or hurting us. Of course, we tend to see ourselves and people we like as high in both. People who we view as high in warmth and low in competence are not "us," but neither are they threatening. We see their shortcomings as misfortune, like the elderly or sick.

A good example of a low-warmth/low-competence view would be how some people see the homeless and very poor: lazy, irresponsible, and undeserving of help or even pity. They are not threatening to us, except perhaps in a vague sense of being a burden on society. Low-warmth/high-competence would apply to people we see as undesirable and dangerous—such as criminals, gang members, and terrorists (or perhaps liberals or conservatives, depending on your own political leanings). Low-warmth/low-competence and low-warmth/high-competence are the categories of "them." Note that in both, the primary excuse for excluding people on these grounds is that they don't care about us (warmth).

When we are interoceptive, connected, and empathic, we develop traits of agreeableness, conscientiousness, and honesty, and we experience reduced mortality rates. Our families have higher levels of stability. When we are kind with each other, we live better lives.

Newburg offers steps for confronting our own biases that we can use for building the "we."

• Become proficient in developing alternative points of view.

• Do not assume that the other person thinks or acts like you.

• Think backward. Instead of thinking about what might happen, put yourself into the future and try to explain how a potential situation could have occurred.

• Imagine that a belief you currently hold is wrong, then develop a scenario to explain how it could be true. This helps you see the limitations of your own beliefs.

• Try out another person's beliefs by acting out the role. This breaks you out of seeing the world through the habitual patterns of your own beliefs.

• Play devil's advocate by taking the minority point of view. This helps you see how alternative assumptions make the world look different.

• Brainstorm. With ideas, quantity leads to quality because the first ones that come to mind are those that reflect old beliefs. New ideas help you to break free of emotional blocks and social norms.

• Interact with people of different backgrounds and beliefs.

Empathy drives us into one of two responses: We can withdraw from the experience, or we can engage. Think of the parable of the Good Samaritan. Two passersby see the beaten man lying on the side of the road but keep walking. The third stops and assists him, even though he is a member of a rival tribe. Empathy in action is compassion. Empathy can be expressed verbally, but compassion can only be demonstrated through action.

We all withdraw sometimes. Compassion can have both clear and hidden costs. Compassion fatigue is common among disaster-relief workers, certain healthcare professionals, and others whose work regularly brings them in contact with people who are suffering. But for most of us, most of the time, the cost is manageable and in the long run is more than offset by the benefits of expanding our group.

There can be valid reasons for excluding. But we have to understand that it's always a choice. More than any other mammal, we have the capacity to be flexible in our distribution of empathy and compassion.

Morality and the Moral Emotions

Morality is not just what's good for me or my group but for the world. It generalizes and broadens, helps us endure pain and hold onto ourselves and each other even as everything else comes apart. Moral emotions—openness, mindfulness, awareness, emotional regulation, and empathy—set the rules, so to speak, for companionship and collaboration and permit the translation of culture, language, and meaning.

Openness is the willingness and desire to step outside of our own, limited perspective and see the world from other points of view. This does not require diminishing one's own experiences but rather recognizing an interconnectedness between them and the experiences of others. It's the opposite of being judgmental. Brain development plays a role in openness, of course, but so does personality. We can choose to be more or less open as we age.

Mindfulness is awareness of the body and mind in the here and now. As I write I am focused on choosing the next few words, but when I pause and look up, I may notice the sounds outside my office or mild back pain from sitting for so long. Mindfulness is impossible when we dwell on the past or speculate about the future. It's important to be in the now to read our bodies because sympathy, empathy, and compassion are body processes.

Awareness of emotional processes is important, but it refers to more than just recognition. Siegel calls it coherence—understanding purposefulness, as well as the cohesiveness of emotions and behaviors. Think of adolescents who are more focused on being part of a group (cohesiveness) than on whether the group is really worth their time (coherence). But we all struggle with this. Accomplishing tasks can make us feel competent but also can leave us feeling empty if the tasks don't provide a sense of purpose.

Emotional regulation is the capacity to experience emotions without being overwhelmed by them. We can navigate the ups and downs of relationships, apologizing and correcting behaviors when necessary (tear and repair). To do this, we need to be able to tolerate shame and still feel "good enough." The alternatives are denial or withdrawal.

These all culminate in the experience of empathy. The word is often misunderstood. Empathy is not simply seeing from another's point of view but understanding another's emotional state. It's also not the same as sympathy, which is a right-brain process. Empathy is a left-brain-to-right-brain transfer, from verbal to visceral and back. And unlike sympathy, empathy does not rely on your having experienced the same things as the other person.

Empathy is imperative for trust. Psychologist Simon Baron-Cohen, an expert in autism and developmental psychopathology, describes empathizing as the ability to predict and care about how others feel.

Empathy is a little more difficult for males. This is evolutionary, a result of human female mate selection.

Many of you will be able to relate to this scenario. Mom hears a noise at night. Dad doesn't. (Women have a lower threshold for reticular activation, especially mothers.) Mom wakes up Dad, who gets up and stumbles toward the possible threat, possibly picking up a weapon of some sort on the way. Mom also gets up and heads straight to the children.

In this situation, Mom is scared and knows it. Dad is scared, too, but doesn't know it, at least not in the same way that Mom does. Dad is focused on his job, confronting the danger. Feelings would only get in the way. As you might have guessed, there is a biological explanation for this: The male corpus callosum tends to be grayer and thinner than females', meaning the flow of information between the hemispheres is less efficient. For obvious reasons, human females would be attracted to mates with this propensity to defy fear and protect the family. We call it compartmentalization. He doesn't have to sort through feelings in order to protect his family from a threat; he just does it.

Incidentally, compartmentalization is also why males will often view emotionally intense situations or relationships as problems to be solved. He asks questions in an effort to gather information that will help him solve the problem. He does not consider or understand that that's not what his female significant other wants. She just wants to be heard and affirmed. This can be intensely frustrating to both partners, the modern downside of the evolutionary advantage.

The Transformational Emotions

The transformational emotions provide a sense of deep, lasting change and are fundamental to human nature. The first of them, hope, is the capacity to believe that change is possible. It can seem nonsensical, but it is vital for human development. The placebo effect is an example of its power.

Altruism is the willingness to share resources with others, even at a cost to oneself, or to use one's strengths and capacities for the greater good. Some have posited that it's selfish: We help others when we can so that others will help us when we need it, or in order to reap the benefits of a reputation for contributing. We do have a propensity to be good to our kin and to others in our group, but true altruism calls on us to aid strangers, too.

Truth is the sense of rightness that we derive from openness, mindfulness, and awareness. And when we understand our world and our place in it, this knowledge grounds us, and we do not feel the need to impose it on others. It's not a sense of rightness, but of "all-rightness."

When we develop our sense of morality, we build narratives around it. These stories reflect "experience and existence with purpose, understanding and comfort with emotional expression," as Siegel puts it. These narratives are the building blocks of culture. (I'm not sure that "purpose, understanding and comfort with emotional expression" is where we are today in our country, but I hope it's where we're headed.)

According to Dr. Judith Landau, neuropsychiatrist and

president of the board of the LINC Foundation, "Feeling connected or attached to family and culture of origins is correlated with reduced risk-taking behaviors, as well as a reduction in family and societal violence, addiction, depression, suicidality, post-traumatic stress and other chronic or life-threating conditions."

We can achieve those attachments by deepening our understanding of one of the traits the separates humans from every other species: our capacity for spirituality.

Building Spiritual Networks

The word *spirituality* is commonly used in discussion of organized religion, but it's broader than that. Spirituality is your sense of interconnectedness with others and how that affects your sense of the future. In *Measuring Spirituality as a Universal Human Experience: A Review of Spirituality Questionnaires*, Eltica de Jager Meezenbroek, et al., describe it as "one's striving for experience or connection with oneself, with others and with nature and a connectedness with the transcendent."

In an article on spirituality in nursing, Dr. Pamela Reed of the University of Arizona defined it as "the propensity to make meaning through a sense or relatedness to dimensions that transcend the self in such a way that empowers and does not devalue the individual." In other words, recognizing that there is something greater than oneself does not require the loss of one's self.

Andrew Newburg, M.D., a neuroscientist at Thomas Jefferson University Hospital, sets these criteria for spirituality:

> The subjective feelings, thoughts, experiences and behaviors that arise from a search or quest for the sacred; the 'search' refers to attempts to identify, articulate, maintain or transform; and the 'sacred' refers to what the individual perceives as a divine being, ultimate reality or ultimate truth.

Newburg's definition of religion, however, includes "a search for non-sacred goals (such as identity, belonging, meaning, health or wellness) in the context of spiritual criteria; and the means and methods of the search receive general validation and support from within an identifiable group of people."

In other words, in Newburg's view, spirituality does not require a concept of God or gods, and religion does not require spirituality. A member of the Veterans of Foreign Wars might get the same fulfillment from participation as a member of the Baptist Church. Obviously, these criteria overlap, and many people are both spiritual and religious. But the distinction between the two is important.

Spirituality grows out of the emotional development that parents provide and can be a late stage of parenting. I'm not insisting that all parenting should lead to a quest for a divine being or ultimate truth. The task of parenting is moral development. But it makes sense to me that an openness to a search for something greater than oneself could follow, or at least a spiritually tolerant perspective. I don't think you can be both emotionally healthy and intolerant of other people's capacity or desire to be spiritual. This narrows the "we."

Spirituality and the hope it can impart are vital to our well-being. Without them, we cannot be truly resilient.

Personally, I believe that if there is a Mind in the universe, an awareness that drives intentionality, that it is so much greater than our minds that it exceeds the difference between the minds of parent and newborn. The parent has no expectation of the newborn except to be. And so I like to believe that the Mind expects no more of us. The power that the Mind has used to create life, at least as represented on Earth, is attachment—from chemical bonds, to procreation, to the relationships that form and sustain us.

Our Stories, Ourselves: The Power of Reading

The 2013 book *Superboys* is a biography of Jerome Siegel and Joe Schuster and the seminal character they created together as teens in the 1930s, Superman. Author Brad Ricca recounts the many influences on the boys that are echoed in the character's story, everything from sci-fi pulp magazines to the bodybuilder-endorsed fitness crazes of the era to the real-life Lois who inspired Superman's future love interest. But one event stands out—the death of Jerry Siegel's father Michel, a Lithuanian immigrant, during a robbery of his clothing store in 1932. Jerry was seventeen.

"Staring at the black marble headstone [one year later] and the tiny black-and-white photo of his father," Ricca writes, "who was both the strongest man he knew and the meekest—who had fainted while being robbed—Jerry wanted to bring his father back as the person he felt he remembered, or should have." The indestructible Superman—and his meek alter ego Clark Kent—made his comic-book debut six years later.

Richard Warshak, professor of psychiatry at the University of Texas Southwestern Medical Center, makes a similar case for the origin of Batman. Writing in *The Atlantic*, Warshak points out an anecdote from Batman co-creator Bob Kane's autobiography, in which he recalls the time, at age fifteen, he was chased and severely beaten by a gang—precisely the kind of crime Batman specialized in preventing. Warshak explains that he was prompted to learn about Batman after noticing that the character "had special appeal to the traumatized children who visited my office."

Fictional characters as real-life saviors. Art imitating life, and vice versa. All mammals communicate, and some display varying levels of self-awareness, but storytelling is a distinctly human trait, involving both ancient and new features of our brains.

Children will pick up language just by listening, but learning to read and write requires effort. Our brains are not built for it. Verbal language is around one hundred thousand years old, and sophisticated grammar about forty thousand. By comparison, reading barely registers on the evolutionary clock. In fact, in most families, you'd only have to go back a few generations to find a time when all of your ancestors were illiterate. So our brains have not quite made the leap to translating graphic imagery into conscious, verbal processes with the same efficiency as grasping nonverbal and verbal communication.

This is why it's crucial to introduce children to reading early, when their neurons are most plastic, and to help them form the habit. Reading and telling stories and making sense of them involve integrative processes of the right and left hemispheres. The left brain drives us to tell logical, linear stories, but the affective right brain is also needed to generate autobiographical memories as well as regulate bodily sensations. In this way, humans can build a coherent and integrated self in connection with their interpersonal networks, enhancing their lives with regulation, connection, and health.

In describing interhemispheric integration, Siegel refers to narrative integration. Humans use stories and narratives to make sense of events, as well as to form social connections with others. Siegel defines narrative integration as the "capacity to observe the self over time, [permitting] us to make sense of our lives as we link the past, present, and the anticipated future."

The advice to read to children, and to encourage them to read, is often couched in terms of helping them learn language and preparing them for school. And reading certainly accomplishes both of those things. But the power of reading goes much deeper. Stories translate culture better than any other tool. They help us understand the mind of someone living hundreds of years ago, or living today but in places we've never visited, amid circumstances we can scarcely imagine. Reading allows us to attune to temperaments that are very different from our own and from the dance partners we discussed earlier. It expands empathic awareness by shifting us from our narrow worlds into others' worlds.

An experiment in Italy found that children who read scenes from *Harry Potter* books that depicted prejudice by unlikeable characters expressed more tolerant attitudes about immigrants than kids who read unrelated scenes. Follow-up studies found similar effects on attitudes toward homosexuals and refugees. An article in *Scientific American* noted, "Literature with complex, developed themes and characters appears to let readers occupy or adopt perspectives they might otherwise not consider; and it seems that [author J. K.] Rowling might get at the beautiful, sobering mess of life in a way that could have a meaningful impact on our children's collective character."

As Alan Bennett put it in his award-winning play *History Boys*, "The best moments in reading are when you come across something—a thought, a feeling, a way of looking at things—which you had thought special and particular to you. Now here it is, set down by someone else, a person you have never met, someone even who is long dead. And it is as if a hand has come out and taken yours."

Visual art is marvelous, but art invites projection. We bring our own experiences and preferences to viewing art, and we may feel things the creator never intended. We do that with reading as well, to some extent, but the storyteller enjoys the advantage of literally spelling out what he or she wants the reader to understand. And that understanding may change one's own thought processes. Writing is the most marvelous and influential creation in our history.

"Cognitive science connects the acquisition of vocabulary to social cognition, or the development of theory of mind—a capacity to attribute mental states, including thoughts, beliefs, and desires, to oneself and other people," writes Lisa Zunshine in *The Chronicle of Higher Education,* advocating for more fiction in the Common Core curriculum. Zunshine is a professor of English at the University of Kentucky who also studies narrative theory as well as cognitive approaches to literary and cultural studies. "Cognitive science thus gives a concrete definition to what proponents of the Common Core standards are seeking for elementary and secondary students: what David Coleman, president of the College Board, calls 'an underlying language of complexity.' It's metacognition—thinking about thinking."

Reading can transform adults as well. Melanie Green, an associate professor of communication at the University of Buffalo with a doctorate in social psychology, researches the power of narrative to change beliefs, including the effects of fictional stories on real-world attitudes. She told the podcast *You Are Not So Smart*, "Narratives are good at helping us step into somebody else's shoes. And so it can evoke our empathy, and that can be used in some prosocial ways, in terms of reducing intergroup negative opinions."

CHAPTER 6

Delivering Impact When and Where It Is Needed

"Hurt people hurt people. That's how pain patterns get passed on, generation after generation after generation. Break the chain today. Meet anger with sympathy, contempt with compassion, cruelty with kindness. Greet grimaces with smiles. Forgive and forget about finding fault. Love is the weapon of the future."

—Yehuda Berg

Resilience is the ability to bounce back from a stressful or traumatizing experience. It depends on a child's perception of safety and protection based on social-emotional ability to self-buffer from the effect of short- or long-term stress. In doing this, children regulate or dysregulate their systems that bring on feelings of fright or helplessness.

Resilience is essential in protecting from and overcoming the adverse effects of toxic stress. For children to build resilience, they need safe, stable, and nurturing homes. They need supportive caregivers who provide care, love, and fun. But what do we do for families in which these developmental essentials are lacking?

Therapy helps, but it's not enough. Verbal processes are secondary to relational processes. The problem with language is it can be invasive. It's not the way you most want to understand you are loved. You want to hear it, but if you don't feel it, if it's not shown relationally, you won't believe it. As we've discussed, we're better equipped for and more reliant on nonverbal communication than we tend to realize. Nonverbal communication—facial expressions, hand gestures, shrugs, posture—drives all of our relationships.

Helping Families Help Themselves with Joy

I was standing in line at McDonald's one day when I noticed a young mother with a toddler in a car-seat carrier. The woman waited for her order, settled at a table, and started to eat—all without once interacting with her child, who remained silent. The woman had done nothing obviously wrong. But it made me wonder: Couldn't moments like this, everyday moments like standing in line or eating a meal, be opportunities for growth and connection?

And what if therapists, caseworkers, and other service providers could show parents ways to use everyday moments to build stronger bonds with their children? What if, instead of giving clients worksheets and checklists, we gave them simple, fun activities to foster play and care with their children almost anywhere, almost any time?

I brought the idea for Joyful Together to the team of therapists in OhioGuidestone's Early Childhood Mental Health department. They embraced the challenge and created activities to appeal to the kids and caregivers they serve—families for whom stress, conflict, and fear are more familiar than lightness and laughter. Those families let us practice with them and learn from them. Along the way, they provided many new ideas. And the results were obvious. Rigid, rule-bound parents relaxed and softened. Oppositional, angry, distrusting children were able to giggle and to stop acting like surly teenagers.

These families' underlying problems didn't disappear, but they were able to find some reprieve. And then they were eager to have more moments of connection. It was the laughter of the adults and children, and their eagerness to keep on playing together, that suggested that we were onto something.

As we've discussed, the hardwired emotional seeking system drives humans towards euphoric experiences—joy—through the building of attachment relationships that provide care, love, and play. When joy is lacking in a family, we can offer a jump start of sorts through activities that facilitate an interpersonal connection between a child and a caregiver.

Care leads to playfulness, play leads to joy, and joy makes for more harmonious homes. Children will obey most of the time when they experience enough joy. When they feel loved and cared for, and when they believe that the love and care will continue indefinitely, they feel hope. Joy and hope, in turn, awaken spirituality. Joy and hope underlie all of the social connections we feel with and for each other and drives us into greater and greater interconnectedness. We allow intuition, trust, and other nonverbal processes to move us into relationships where we will experience joy and hope repeatedly. That's a spiritual network. There is virtually no limit to the power of these forces to transform individuals, families, and whole communities.

By helping parents and caregivers regain control of their

own heightened stress-response processes, we can help them become a source of emotional co-regulation and support for their children. But we need to change the focus from "teaching" caregivers how to parent to "practicing" the act of parenting with them. When we teach, we activate the word-based, linear left brain, which has a limited link to the rest of the body and its processes. When we *practice*, we can elicit the emotional right brain and work to calm the response system. By actively practicing this in therapy, caregivers can begin to learn how to co-regulate directly from the experience in the right brain, rather than learning a step-by-step, word-based method as if it were from a textbook. As the right brain practices co-regulation, caregivers can begin practicing it at home with their own children.

OhioGuidestone's Joyful Together activities comprise a relationship-centered therapy technique based on sensory experiences. Anyone can do it, almost anywhere and almost anytime. It's fun and effective. Our manual for mental health professionals provides more than a hundred examples of activities, plus tips for how to adapt them or create your own. These activities are organized around the five sensory experiences—touch, taste, hearing, sight, and smell—plus two more categories: hugging and balance. Most activities do not require any materials, and all are easy to do. The simple goal is to promote positive and happy interpersonal play between caregivers and their children. The end result is more secure attachments, more effective co-regulation, more successful emotional development—and authentic joy.

The five senses, plus balance and hugging, were chosen as points of entries for the Joyful Together activities because they are easily incorporated into everyday life without many tools.

Further, sensory experiences are heightened through interpersonal experiences and sensory play and are critical for healthy brain development. Young children learn with all of their senses and are wired to receive and utilize sensory input beginning in the womb. Initiating play around touch, taste, hearing, sight, and smell promotes cognitive, language, social emotional, and physical development, and the overall neurobiological experience of joy.

Balance, or proprioception, was also chosen as a point of entry because it allows children to monitor risk and safety. When children have a little bit of "danger" within the safe context of play, joy processes are elicited. Children are able to accurately deduce what is and what is not really threatening and can practice regulating their stress response systems.

Hugging was added as a point of entry as well because human touch directly calms affective body processes and is beneficial to relationship processes and attunement. Hugging triggers co-regulation and downplays one's activated systems. Hugs prompt a mind-body experience of safety and release endorphins in the brain. Hugs slow breath and heart rates and produce good feelings that humans seek through care and love.

The key to all of the activities is making sure that parents and children understand that there is no "right way" to play. Play is guided by rules that differ from person to person and from activity to activity.

Some examples of Joyful Together activities:

• Mirror Mirror: Caregiver and child sit face-to-face and try to be each other's "mirror" by imitating the facial expressions, movements, and posture of one another.

• Cloud Party: Adult asks the child to watch the clouds "have a party" in the sky and imagine silly details. "Who are the guests? A big, fat hippo? A long, skinny weasel? And what are they doing up there? If you were up in the sky with the clouds, which one would you ride on?"

• Copy Cat Rhythm: Caregiver prompts the child to watch and listen, then claps or taps a rhythm that the child is able to imitate. The child then gets to tap a rhythm for the adult to copy. This can be done with other sounds, too.

• Baker's Square: Cooking together can be an extremely rewarding and bonding experience. Let the child make decisions about what to make, when to stir, etc. Children love to feel that they are in charge of a process.

• Animal Kisses: Adult and child take turns imitating how animals would approach each other and kiss.

• Stop and Go: The adult announces that it's time for tickles, but the child determines when the adult starts and stops. Then they switch roles.

Joyful Together activities are simple, variable, and require little or no preparation.

All parents have days when they feel too tired, distracted, or stressed to engage playfully with their children. In households besieged by toxic stress, the parents may feel that way all or most of the time. These activities are intended to help them get back in touch with the seeking instincts that have been overwhelmed by stress.

Helping Parents and Other Caregivers

Even four million years ago, we were the smartest mammals on Earth. But how did our brains work? We communicated nonverbally. Our nonverbal communication may have been even more sophisticated than it is today. As we've evolved, it's possible that we've lost some of that nonverbal processing. But as Allan Schore notes, we're still right-brain dominant. We act on our feelings much more than we ever realize. And because those processes are nonverbal, they're largely outside our awareness.

If I were explaining this to you in person, you would likely maintain eye contact and nod slightly while you listened, nonverbal cues that you're engaged. You wouldn't have to think about nodding; mirror neurons in your right hemisphere would just quietly send the signal to the appropriate muscles. But then if I pointed out that you were nodding, you would become aware of it, and it would start to feel awkward. Or you might try to stop. Either way, you'd be focusing on something that you weren't a moment before. That's because I moved it from your right brain to your left brain, to your awareness.

That's an example of what we need to do for people struggling with affective, negative experiences. We try to move those into conscious awareness so that they can discuss them and learn how their unconscious processes are driving them. This is especially important for relationships. Parents and children, husbands and wives, can set each other off, over and over again, with nonverbal cues. They are communicating right brain to right brain, probably without realizing it, unaware of how they constantly tear the relationship. If we can help them move these habits into their awareness, we can help them repair the relationship.

That's what joy does. Joy provides positive experiences and new words, which helps them change the nonverbal cues and avoid the constant tearing. We use the new skills of the left brain to shine a light on ancient, mysterious processes of the right brain.

The movement from right brain to left brain is not easy. There is a language barrier, so to speak, in that one of the parties in this dialogue does not speak. The hemispheres coordinate, but they fundamentally do not understand each other. If they were people and the left brain were to ask, "What's bothering you?", the right brain might respond with abstract art or music. The left brain is verbal; the right brain is imagistic. The left brain is explicit; the right brain is implicit. The left brain is sequential; the right brain is experiential. The left brain looks at the night sky and names the constellations and the planets; the right brain stares in awe at the beautiful, terrible vastness of space.

Shame is nonverbal and focused on the past. Hope is related to the future and therefore verbal; we need words to think or talk about what we expect or want to happen. Your planning will not connect to your shame. But to overcome the reluctance that comes with shame, you have to imagine the future around what has shamed you, around your inadequacies. In other words, you need to think about things you really don't want to think about. We don't daydream about challenges; we daydream about how things could be if or when we overcome our challenges. We all have a natural reluctance to worry about hardship. But that's the discipline it takes. It's like wanting to be thin but not wanting to work out or eat better.

When trying to bring hope to someone who's wracked with shame, we use an imaginary "helper" in a process called Story Building. It equips them to confront shame by imagining that someone is there to offer guidance and support in the same way that a parent or partner would be in a healthy relationship. This helps them bring the light of hope into the dark corners where their shame hides.

In Story Building Therapy, the aim is to relieve feelings of shame through the use of personal narratives around particularly shameful experiences and, within that narrative, create a "Helper," or change agent, who says and does things within the narrative that craft a better story for the client. Through activation of the emotional and creative right brain, the affective link to the body's stress systems helps the person experience calmness. The intervention moves the client beyond self-awareness to insight and into the realm of therapeutic experiences that heal the wound of shame and insufficiency. By creating a new experience of the self and increasing affect regulation, the SBT process ultimately inspires hope.

To begin, the person focuses on recounting an incident, recalling who was there, what took place, when it happened, and where the event occurred. The clinician listens for clues revealing the emotions driving the story and for opportunities to move into the second phase. In Story Building, the clinician asks the client to retell the story in the present tense, but this time imagining a Helper who could have been there to make the story different. The Helper's role is not to disengage the client from what really happened but to offer some relief from the shame associated with the event. The clinician encourages the client to describe what the Helper is saying and doing.

After the building process is complete, the next step is for the clinician to encourage and lead the client to reflect upon the changes in the story and the impact the changes have had on the client's experience of self. The focus here is not on who the Helper is, but what the Helper says and does, and how the addition of the Helper enabled a change within the personal narrative.

Another OhioGuidestone therapy, Integrative Nar-ART-ives, also builds on stories, but ones provided to the client. In Integrative Nar-ART-ives, the clinician reads a guided-imagery narrative to the client, provides a drawing prompt based on the narrative, then asks questions designed to help the client verbally process feelings associated with steps one and two. The narrative and drawing activities work in the affective right brain, where emotional problems live. Then, language is carefully used to move and process those emotions in the left brain, completely integrating the entire brain and the body as one.

An example:

> Take a deep and slow breath. Slowly let go of it. As you breathe out, feel your body resting comfortably in your chair. Feel your feet on the ground, your arms and hands in your lap. Breathe slowly and comfortably. Let go of your worries about your breath. Just breathe as your body wants to. If you can, close your eyes. Breathe calmly and naturally.
>
> Imagine yourself walking in the woods, trying to recover from a hard day full of troubles. You are tired. You are exhausted. You don't want to have another argument, another fight, or another meeting about things you should have done or things you should not have done. You just need a place to rest and recover. A place of your own where no one can find you unless you want to be found. A place where no one can hurt you.
>
> As you continue on your walk, the forest sends gentle leaves your way. A single leaf lands on your shoulder, then dances in front of you as if to lead you. Curious, you follow

until you stand in front of a majestic fortress protected by a wall covered with a thick layer of green vines. You stretch out your hand to touch the wall and your leaf lands in your outstretched hand. As it lands, the leaf turns into a key. The vines part in front of you and a door appears.

You use your key. You enter the fortress. You close the door behind you and the vines cover the door again. You walk across a drawbridge into the courtyard of your fortress. A table is set for you and you eat: Fresh baked bread, a bowl of fragrant soup, a crisp apple. It is a simple meal, but you enjoy every bite of it. You feel strength and clarity of mind returning to you.

You rise from the table to explore the fortress. You decide to climb the spiral staircase leading up one of the four towers marking the four corners of your fortress. It is a long climb up the stairs, but when you reach the top you can see farther than you could ever imagine. You can see the courtyard and you can see the place where you started your walk. You can see the city in the distance. You can see people, lots of them, walking in the city and a few of them in the forest. You can see roads, building, and rivers. You can see the world.

From up here in the tower, everything down there seems small and less troublesome. Surely someone down there is having another argument, another fight, and another meeting about things that should be done and things that should not be done. None of this matters up here in the tower. You are protected from the troubles of the world. You can see what you want to see. You can turn away from things you do not want to see. You can climb up another staircase and look at another corner of the world. This is your fortress. It protects you. You can leave here and come back any time you need to.

When you are ready, slowly open your eyes, breathe, and look around. You are back here, in the room, but the feeling of protection and strength is still with you.

Now take a piece of paper and a few colored pencils/ crayons of your choice and draw your fortress. Imagine and draw the wall surrounding the fortress. It is covered in vines. Draw the door that leads to your fortress. You may even want to draw the leaf that became a key to your fortress. Draw your fortress with the four towers. Think about how high they are. Draw yourself in the fortress anywhere you want. You may also want to draw some of the forest and the land surrounding your fortress.

After allowing a few minutes for drawing, the clinician asks questions, such as: How high are the towers of your fortress? What do you think it would feel like to be able to see everything surrounding you? Have you ever wanted to hide from the world? When you need to hide, where do you go? Or who do you go to? Do you think it is OK to feel and be overwhelmed and need a break? If you could give one person a key to your fortress and a map for finding it, who would it be? Who would you want to hide the key from?

By bridging the gap between brain hemispheres with images and words, clients can build libraries of positive images that they can carry with them and use in times of need. The intention is not to erase or replace the images that already live in the right brain, but rather add to them.

CHAPTER 7

Investing in the (Human) Bond Market

"I know in my heart that man is good, that what is right will always eventually triumph, and there is purpose and worth to each and every life."

—President Ronald Reagan

As I was wrapping up the first draft of this book, I came across a news story about a formerly homeless teenage boy from Philadelphia who'd just earned a full scholarship to Harvard. Stories like this are inspiring; Americans love underdogs. But even as I quietly cheered for this young man, I couldn't help but think about the countless others left behind.

The Atlantic contributor David H. Freedman addressed this ambivalence in a 2016 essay bluntly titled "The War on Stupid People: American society increasingly mistakes intelligence for human worth":

> Confronted with evidence that our approach [to education] is failing—high-school seniors reading at the fifth-grade level, abysmal international rankings—we comfort ourselves with the idea that we're taking steps to locate

> those underprivileged kids who are, against the odds, extremely intelligent. Finding this tiny minority of gifted poor children and providing them with exceptional educational opportunities allows us to conjure the evening-news-friendly fiction of an equal-opportunity system, as if the problematically ungifted majority were not as deserving of attention as the "overlooked gems."

In 2012, the Brookings Institute tackled the subject of opportunity—and lack of it—in the report *Pathways to the Middle Class: Balancing Personal and Public Responsibilities.*

> Americans are more comfortable with the idea of increasing opportunities for success than with reducing inequality. When the American public is asked questions about the importance of tackling each, a far higher proportion is in favor of doing something about ensuring that more people have a shot at climbing the economic ladder than is in favor of reducing poverty or inequality.

The problem is, these are not separate issues. The game may not be rigged, exactly, but clearly some people step onto the field far better equipped and trained to play than others.

The Brookings report explains:

> Children from less advantaged families tend to fall behind at every stage. They are less likely to be ready for school at age 5 (59% vs 72%), to achieve core academic and social competencies at the end of elementary school (60% vs 77%), to graduate from high school with decent grades and no involvement with crime or teen pregnancy (41% vs

> 70%), and to graduate from college or achieve the equivalent income in their twenties (48% vs 70%). Racial gaps are large from the start and never narrow significantly, especially for African Americans, who trail by an average of 25 percentage points for the identified benchmarks.
>
> There are not just large but widening gaps by socioeconomic status in family formation patterns, test scores, college going, and adult earnings. These gaps should be addressed or the nation risks becoming increasingly divided over time.

To the extent that we discuss opportunity at all, the debate never gets past one simple assertion, repeated like a mantra and accepted by many as immutable fact: We can't afford to help everyone.

But what about the cost—to all of us—of not helping? This is not just a moral question, but an economic one. There are tangible, measurable benefits to helping people live better.

In 2017, the news site Slate.com partnered with the Hechinger Report and the Teacher Project, nonprofit news organizations focused on education coverage, for a series called "The Trouble with Two." The series calls attention to the developmental needs of two-year-olds and how little our society does to support their families. A single paragraph from one article (titled "Can We Improve America by Taking Better Care of Our 2-Year-Olds?") neatly laid out some of the cascading—and self-perpetuating—effects of this failure:

> The size of a child's vocabulary at age 2 can predict his academic and behavioral abilities at the start of kindergarten. School readiness at the start of kindergarten can affect a

> child's ability to read by third grade. Kids who read by third grade are more likely to graduate from high school. People who graduate from high school have higher earnings and are less likely to end up in jail. Parents who aren't in jail and who have the capacity to earn a living wage are more likely to have children with larger vocabularies by age 2.

Now imagine how many billions of dollars, in direct costs and untapped potential, are represented in those few sentences. Then factor in health care. You may recall the CDC and Kaiser Permanente report that noted that adverse childhood experiences (ACEs) have been linked to the ten leading causes of death in the United States. That report went on to state: "The impact of ACEs is felt not only in health care, but also in businesses because of employee absenteeism, in homelessness, and in the criminal justice system. ACEs likely cost untold billions of dollars a year."

There is no line for these costs on our paycheck stubs or on the 1040 form, but every taxpayer is on the hook for them.

A 2009 report from researchers at the University of Dublin and published in the journal *Economics and Human Biology* made a fiscal-responsibility case for helping families and pre-school-age children: "Early investment in preventive programmes aimed at disadvantaged children is often more cost effective than later remediation. By investing early, the benefits are larger and are enjoyed for longer, which in turn increases the return to investment. The economic argument for early investment does not preclude later investment; rather it argues that there are dynamic complementarities to be gained from investing at different stages of the life cycle, starting as early as possible."

An American experiment bears this out. In the 1990s, the U.S. Department of Housing and Urban Development launched a program called Move to Opportunity (MTO) in five cities. Thousands of families living in typical public housing projects were offered either a standard Section 8 voucher to rent a home or a voucher that could be used only in a census tract with a poverty rate below 10 percent—an upper-middle-class community. The program lasted four years.

In 2015, researchers at Harvard looked again at the MTO data and followed up with the families that had relocated to more affluent communities. They found that contrary to previous assertions, the families enjoyed not just improved physical and mental health, but the children went on to earn more money. There was one caveat, however: The child's age at the time of the move mattered.

Among those who were teens when they moved, the income differences were statistically insignificant. For those eight and under, however, they estimated an increase in lifetime earnings of more than three hundred thousand dollars.

"The additional tax revenue generated from these earnings increases would itself offset the incremental cost of the subsidized voucher relative to providing public housing," the researchers wrote. "We conclude that offering low-income families housing vouchers and assistance in moving to lower-poverty neighborhoods has substantial benefits for the families themselves and for taxpayers. . . . More broadly, our findings suggest that efforts to integrate disadvantaged families into mixed-income communities are likely to reduce the persistence of poverty across generations."

The report does not address the level of "not in my backyard" resistance the MTO program generated or would generate if replicated today. But smaller investments would yield smaller, but still beneficial results.

Researchers in Philadelphia recently added to the large body of evidence that access to green space has a measurable effect on people's mental and physical health. In an experiment, they cleaned and beautified some abandoned lots in the city, simply cleaned others by removing debris, and left other lots as they were, over-grown and trash-strewn, for a control group.

As NPR reported: "The team surveyed residents living near the lots before and after their trial to assess their mental health and wellbeing. . . . People living near the newly greened lots felt better. . . . The impact was strongest for residents of poorer neighborhoods—they showed at least a 27.5 percent reduction in the prevalence of depression."

Ming Kuo, an associate professor at the University of Illinois' Department of Natural Resources and Environmental Sciences, has found similar results in Chicago. She explained on the Hidden Brain podcast that in surveys of residents of public housing facilities with varying levels of greenery nearby, "we found social breakdown in buildings without trees and grass around them. That is to say, when we asked people did they know their neighbors, did they speak to their neighbors, do they know them on first-name basis, could they rely on their neighbors for, you know, for a favor, to take care of their kids if they had an emergency, then the people in the buildings with a bit of greenery were much more likely to say yes. We also found that the folks who are in the less-green buildings are reporting more aggressive behaviors." Police reports also showed higher numbers of calls to the less-green sites.

"There's this attention restoration theory, which says that when people don't have access to nature, they're going to be more mentally fatigued," Kuo explained. "So when you're mentally fatigued, you're also less good at handling difficult social situations."

"When you look out at a green landscape, even from indoors, your heart rate will go down, and you'll change from . . . what we call 'fight or flight' into 'tend and befriend' mode. So it has these very systematic physiological impacts on us, which we also know have long-term health outcomes associated with them."

Kuo's research has also shown that school children learn more and behave better when some classes are held outside in a natural setting (more natural, at least, than their classroom). The benefits can be seen even after they go back indoors. And this is separate from the growing body of research showing that increasing recess time improves academic performance by venting some of the pressure that builds when children are forced to fight their powerful natural urges to move and play.

Trauma-Informed Policies

At OhioGuidestone, many of our clients have experienced trauma. More than half recall four or more adverse childhood experiences (ACEs). Many still experience conditions of toxic stress related to marginalization, discrimination, and poverty, as well as trauma that occurred in the recent or distant past. This is why we are a leader in advancing trauma-informed care in Ohio. We have trained more than a thousand clinicians across the state, and our Joyful Together interventions (described in Chapter 6) are now used in hundreds of schools and early education and childcare centers.

With every client, we ask: What happened to you? What got you to this point? What conditions contributed to this crisis? This assists with removing blame and shame and also signals that we are respectful of client contexts. We understand that our clients may have a heightened response to stress, and that we must interact in ways that reduce the client's sense of danger in our presence. These responses are unique. Trauma and toxic stress affect everyone differently, and even an individual's response can change over time. We cannot change people's experiences, but we—all of us—can change how we help them.

Ohio Avenue Elementary School, located in one of Columbus' poorest neighborhoods, is taking a different approach to behavior issues among its stressed-out students. "Every adult in the building has received training on how children respond to trauma," according to an article in *The Atlantic*.

> They've come to understand how trauma can make kids emotionally volatile and prone to misinterpret accidental bumps or offhand remarks as hostile. They've learned how to de-escalate conflict, and to interpret misbehavior not as a personal attack or an act of defiance. And they're perennially looking for new ways to help the kids manage their overwhelming feelings and control their impulses.
>
> "If the focus is on what the adults are doing, that's where you get the bang for your buck. We can control what the adults do," explained Olympia Della Flora, the school's principal, when I visited this spring. "How are [the children] going to learn a positive way of dealing with conflict if we're not the ones showing it?"

The school received an A for progress on most of its recent annual report cards. As the article's author asked, "What if the most effective way to help kids learn self-control is for adults to stop being so controlling?"

In Pennsylvania, two legislators—a Republican and a Democrat—have proposed trauma-informed training for all teachers and school employees in the state, using a tiny portion of the $60 million already designated for school safety.

In Cleveland, where OhioGuidestone is based, MetroHealth System has partnered with local faith leaders to form the Community Trauma Institute. The goal is to train church-based "trauma responders," who will follow up with people after treatment at a MetroHealth hospital. Long-term plans call for training community members to spot the signs of anxiety, depression, and toxic stress and to guide sufferers to resources.

The initiative is spearheaded by the Rev. Dr. Tony Minor, who wrote a moving essay for the Cleveland *Plain Dealer* after the school shooting in Parkland, Florida, mentioning some of the violent crimes that happened in Cleveland around the same time but received little or no attention.

> The folks living in the neighborhoods where these everyday horrors occur hear the gunshots, sirens and screams, they see the body bags, they live in fear. This is trauma, too. Is it any less than what the shattered souls in Parkland experienced?
>
> Until recently, we didn't think about "community trauma"—the collective damage caused by everyday exposure to violence, crime, poverty, blight, delinquency and disinvestment. This trauma is insidious because it harms

not only individuals, it tears apart a community's social fabric, ripping residents away from trust, hope and health. Community trauma is now not only widely recognized by medical professionals, it is an epidemic.

And like all epidemics, its causes can be determined, its spread contained and its symptoms treated. We lack only the collective will.

Empathy and Leadership

We live in fractious times. We seem to be so good at and comfortable with tribal warfare that it's fair to wonder if this is just who we are. In his novel *Freedom*, Jonathan Franzen remarks that the "American experiment in self-government" was "statistically skewed from the outset, because it wasn't the people with sociable genes who fled the crowded Old World for the new continent; it was the people who didn't get along well with others."

But it doesn't have to be this way. Leadership matters.

Pack animals, like wolves, have a significant hierarchical structure with dominance. The alpha establishes and protects his role through aggression. His rights may include eating first or the most, but his responsibilities include leading the hunt and keeping the pack safe.

Among group mammals—the great apes and humans—the hierarchy resolves internal conflicts. The alpha male in a chimp community or the alpha female in a bonobo clan will settle squabbles. Group mammals also have the most sophisticated empathic processes because relationships are vital to survival.

Researchers have noticed that chimps are more likely to share food with those who groomed them earlier. All of this, according to de Waal, shows that group mammals—including humans—are hardwired to be emotionally attuned, and that that attunement drives behavior. Emotional processing driving behavior that causes us to treat each other better forms the substrates of moral development.

In group mammals, moral development is the function of the leadership of the group, to define who the "we" is, and to help them get along. But as humans, we have great flexibility in this and in how we treat those like us and those who are different.

Joshua Greene, a Harvard-based philosopher and experimental psychologist, monitored the brain activity of people who were asked to solve challenging moral dilemmas. For example: There's a train rushing down the track and it's going to kill five people, but you can pull a switch that will divert the train to another track where it will kill one person. These are the only options. What do you do? Most people choose the second track and single death.

But then he alters the situation slightly. This time the only way to save the five people is to push a large man onto the track. The numbers of potential fatalities are the same as in the first scenario, but people have a much harder time choosing to cause one person's death than they do just allowing it to happen. In his experiment, Greene found that the right brain was activated as the participants struggled with this question. And remember, the right brain is nonverbal and is most shaped by our relational histories.

This is why we can't rely solely on logic, reason, or any other word-based appeal on people regarding their in-group and out-group boundaries. And we certainly can't bully or ridicule them into it. If you want to change someone's mind, you have to engage in a relationship with them. You have to become their friend and engage in shared activities. You have to express empathy and show compassion.

And leaders at all levels—parents and teachers, ministers, influential business executives, elected and appointed officials—must participate.

We have a long history of fighting over group membership. America was born in a war over this, and a century later half a million people died in an internal conflict over identities and personhood. We've seen time and again that this debate is fraught with danger if we don't understand the moral kindness that even our closest evolutionary cousins do. We're supposed to treat each other gently. Our leaders are supposed to resolve conflicts, not exacerbate them. We're supposed to enlarge our group, not reduce it. There is a moral imperative in our evolutionary heritage that should drive us toward building together. When we fail, we undermine not just our own lives, but the lives of those who come after us.

I'm not trying to suggest that any of this would be easy. Modern economists have amassed an enormous amount of evidence that we are not the "rational actors" that past theorists liked to imagine. We are hardwired to worry about our resources and to respond strongly to threats, real and imagined. But we used to be pretty good at taking a long view and trusting each other, and I believe we can do it again. As the late Senator Paul Wellstone used to say, "We all do better when we all do better."

In the introduction to this book, I noted that I was writing for mental health professionals, for people who make policy and funding decisions that determine where and how resources are allocated, and for concerned citizens everywhere. I'd like to close with some general advice for each group.

Therapists: If you take away anything from this book, let it be that whatever your training and discipline, all of our interventions must be relational. Our species thrived because of our unique capacity to be understood and to understand, to be loved and to love (to paraphrase the Prayer of St. Francis), and we are stuck with each other, for better or worse. The resilience necessary to recover from trauma and cope with stress is learned in, and rejuvenated by, relationships. There is no other source. Learn as much as you can about neuroscience and keep abreast of new developments; biology is now as vital to your work as psychology.

Decision-makers: Take the time to understand what community mental health providers and their clients face every day. Listen patiently to those on the front lines, and encourage your peers to do the same. Support those programs and policies that offer families and communities opportunities to develop the skills they need for the long term. This may require you to re-assess how—and when—you measure success. Every situation, every decision is different, of course, but every program seeking support should be able to demonstrate that, whatever the specifics of its offerings, it bolsters resilience in the people it serves. Above all, remember that empathy doesn't always come naturally to us. We have to keep practicing, and setting examples for others.

The community at large: Never underestimate the power of small actions. Get involved in your own community, or in one that seems to need help, in whatever way you can, for however long you can. Practice "random acts of kindness," as the bumper sticker suggests. Joe Wilson, the formerly homeless man who is now the executive director of the Hospitality House in San Francisco, put it this way in an interview on *PBS News Hour*: "A momentary glance, a touch, a smile, any evidence of human warmth makes a huge difference in people's lives. And it certainly made a huge difference in mine, when someone was willing to make eye contact with me, was willing to actually touch me as another human being. That had more value than a dollar. . . . I would hope that we could remind ourselves that it is the judgment and the harshness in our eyes that really make an imprint on those who have nothing."

Acknowledgments

I would like to express my sincerest appreciation to OhioGuidestone, particularly to Rich Frank, president and CEO, and the board of directors for their guidance and support for this project. To the many staff at OhioGuidestone and the Fellows at the Institute of Family and Community Impact, thank you so much for your input as we work to reduce the effects of trauma and stress in the lives of our clients. You are too numerous to list, and I am sure that I would accidentally leave someone off the list of names.

I especially thank Andrew Garner, MD, an OhioGuidestone Board member, for his willingness to read an early version of the text and offer his helpful feedback.

Working with Frank W. Lewis, the writing partner who took our ideas and vision and translated them to paper, has been a joy and I know that this project would not have happened without him. David Gray's publishing expertise and ability to juggle multiple projects has been amazing to watch.

More than my family will ever know, they are responsible for my growth and learning. I am better because of all of them.

Finally, my deepest love and appreciation to my wife, who, without even trying, entirely rewired my 10th cranial "vagus" nerve and the right hemisphere of my brain. My life is an amazing spectrum of color and texture because of her. Hally, I love you!